Essential
Understanding
Series

Developing
Essential Understanding
of
Functions

for Teaching Mathematics *in*
Grades 9–12

Thomas J. Cooney
University of Georgia
Athens, Georgia

Sybilla Beckmann
University of Georgia
Athens, Georgia

Gwendolyn M. Lloyd
The Pennsylvania State University
University Park, Pennsylvania

Patricia S. Wilson
Volume Editor
University of Georgia
Athens, Georgia

Rose Mary Zbiek
Series Editor
The Pennsylvania State University
University Park, Pennsylvania

NATIONAL COUNCIL OF
TEACHERS OF MATHEMATICS

Library of Congress Cataloging-in-Publication Data

Developing an essential understanding of functions for teaching mathematics
in grades 9-12 / Thomas J. Cooney ... [et al.].
    p. cm. -- (Essential understanding series)
  Includes bibliographical references.
  ISBN 978-0-87353-623-3
  1. Functions--Study and teaching (Secondary) 2. Mathematics--Study and
teaching (Secondary) 3. Curriculum enrichment. I. Cooney, Thomas J.
  QA331.D555 2010
  510.71'2--dc22

2010027248

The National Council of Teachers of Mathematics is the public voice of mathematics education,
supporting teachers to ensure equitable mathematics learning of the highest quality for all
students through vision, leadership, professional development, and research.

Printed in the United States of America

Contents

Chapter 3 93
Challenges: Learning, Teaching, and Assessing

References 107

Foreword

Teaching mathematics in prekindergarten–grade 12 requires a special understanding of mathematics. Effective teachers of mathematics think about and beyond the content that they teach, seeking explanations and making connections to other topics, both inside and outside mathematics. Students meet curriculum and achievement expectations when they work with teachers who know what mathematics is important for each topic that they teach.

The National Council of Teachers of Mathematics (NCTM) presents the Essential Understanding Series in tandem with a call to focus the school mathematics curriculum in the spirit of *Curriculum Focal Points for Prekindergarten through Grade 8 Mathematics: A Quest for Coherence*, published in 2006, and *Focus in High School Mathematics: Reasoning and Sense Making*, released in 2009. The Essential Understanding books are a resource for individual teachers and groups of colleagues interested in engaging in mathematical thinking to enrich and extend their own knowledge of particular mathematics topics in ways that benefit their work with students. The topic of each book is an area of mathematics that is difficult for students to learn, challenging to teach, and critical for students' success as learners and in their future lives and careers.

Drawing on their experiences as teachers, researchers, and mathematicians, the authors have identified the big ideas that are at the heart of each book's topic. A set of essential understandings–mathematical points that capture the essence of the topic–fleshes out each big idea. Taken collectively, the big ideas and essential understandings give a view of a mathematics that is focused, connected, and useful to teachers. Links to topics that students encounter earlier and later in school mathematics and to instruction and assessment practices illustrate the relevance and importance of a teacher's essential understanding of mathematics.

On behalf of the Board of Directors, I offer sincere thanks and appreciation to everyone who has helped to make this series possible. I extend special thanks to Rose Mary Zbiek for her leadership as series editor. I join the Essential Understanding project team in welcoming you to these books and in wishing you many years of continued enjoyment of learning and teaching mathematics.

Henry Kepner
President, 2008–2010
National Council of Teachers of Mathematics

Preface

From prekindergarten through grade 12, the school mathematics curriculum includes important topics that are pivotal in students' development. Students who understand these ideas cross smoothly into new mathematical terrain and continue moving forward with assurance.

However, many of these topics have traditionally been challenging to teach as well as learn, and they often prove to be barriers rather than gateways to students' progress. Students who fail to get a solid grounding in them frequently lose momentum and struggle in subsequent work in mathematics and related disciplines.

The Essential Understanding Series identifies such topics at all levels. Teachers who engage students in these topics play critical roles in students' mathematical achievement. Each volume in the series invites teachers who aim to be not just proficient but outstanding in the classroom—teachers like you—to enrich their understanding of one or more of these topics to ensure students' continued development in mathematics.

How much do you need to know?

To teach these challenging topics effectively, you must draw on a mathematical understanding that is both broad and deep. The challenge is to know considerably more about the topic than you expect your students to know and learn.

Why does your knowledge need to be so extensive? Why must it go above and beyond what you need to teach and your students need to learn? The answer to this question has many parts.

To plan successful learning experiences, you need to understand different models and representations and, in some cases, emerging technologies as you evaluate curriculum materials and create lessons. As you choose and implement learning tasks, you need to know what to emphasize and why those ideas are mathematically important.

While engaging your students in lessons, you must anticipate their perplexities, help them avoid known pitfalls, and recognize and dispel misconceptions. You need to capitalize on unexpected classroom opportunities to make connections among mathematical ideas. If assessment shows that students have not understood the material adequately, you need to know how to address weaknesses that you have identified in their understanding. Your understanding must be sufficiently versatile to allow you to represent the mathematics in different ways to students who don't understand it the first time. In addition, you need to know where the topic fits in the full span of the mathematics curriculum. You must understand where your students are coming from in their thinking and where they are heading mathematically in the months and years to come.

Accomplishing these tasks in mathematically sound ways is a tall order. A rich understanding of the mathematics supports the varied work of teaching as you guide your students and keep their learning on track.

How can the Essential Understanding Series help?

The Essential Understanding books offer you an opportunity to delve into the mathematics that you teach and reinforce your content knowledge. They do not include materials for you to use directly with your students, nor do they discuss classroom management, teaching styles, or assessment techniques. Instead, these books focus squarely on issues of mathematical content—the ideas and understanding that you must bring to your preparation, in-class instruction, one-on-one interactions with students, and assessment.

How do the authors approach the topics?

For each topic, the authors identify "big ideas" and "essential understandings." The big ideas are mathematical statements of overarching concepts that are central to a mathematical topic and link numerous smaller mathematical ideas into coherent wholes. The books call the smaller, more concrete ideas that are associated with each big idea *essential understandings*. They capture aspects of the corresponding big idea and provide evidence of its richness.

The big ideas have tremendous value in mathematics. You can gain an appreciation of the power and worth of these densely packed statements through persistent work with the interrelated essential understandings. Grasping these multiple smaller concepts and through them gaining access to the big ideas can greatly increase your intellectual assets and classroom possibilities.

In your work with mathematical ideas in your role as a teacher, you have probably observed that the essential understandings are often at the heart of the understanding that you need for presenting one of these challenging topics to students. Knowing these ideas very well is critical because they are the mathematical pieces that connect to form each big idea.

How are the books organized?

Every book in the Essential Understanding Series has the same structure:

- The introduction gives an overview, explaining the reasons for the selection of the particular topic and highlighting some of the differences between what teachers and students need to know about it.

- Chapter 1 is the heart of the book, identifying and examining the big ideas and related essential understandings.

Big ideas and essential understandings are identified by icons in the books.

marks a big idea, and

marks an essential understanding.

- Chapter 2 reconsiders the ideas discussed in chapter 1 in light of their connections with mathematical ideas within the grade band and with other mathematics that the students have encountered earlier or will encounter later in their study of mathematics.

- Chapter 3 wraps up the discussion by considering the challenges that students often face in grasping the necessary concepts related to the topic under discussion. It analyzes the development of their thinking and offers guidance for presenting ideas to them and assessing their understanding.

The discussion of big ideas and essential understandings in chapter 1 is interspersed with questions labeled "Reflect." It is important to pause in your reading to think about these on your own or discuss them with your colleagues. By engaging with the material in this way, you can make the experience of reading the book participatory, interactive, and dynamic.

Reflect questions can also serve as topics of conversation among local groups of teachers or teachers connected electronically in school districts or even between states. Thus, the Reflect items can extend the possibilities for using the books as tools for formal or informal experiences for in-service and preservice teachers, individually or in groups, in or beyond college or university classes.

marks a "Reflect" question that appears on a different page.

A new perspective

The Essential Understanding Series thus is intended to support you in gaining a deep and broad understanding of mathematics that can benefit your students in many ways. Considering connections between the mathematics under discussion and other mathematics that students encounter earlier and later in the curriculum gives the books unusual depth as well as insight into vertical articulation in school mathematics.

The series appears against the backdrop of *Principles and Standards for School Mathematics* (NCTM 2000), *Curriculum Focal Points for Prekindergarten through Grade 8 Mathematics: A Quest for Coherence* (NCTM 2006), *Focus in High School Mathematics: Reasoning and Sense Making* (NCTM 2009), and the Navigations Series (NCTM 2001–2009). The new books play an important role, supporting the work of these publications by offering content-based professional development.

The other publications, in turn, can flesh out and enrich the new books. After reading this book, for example, you might select hands-on, Standards-based activities from the Navigations books for your students to use to gain insights into the topics that the Essential Understanding books discuss. If you are teaching students in prekindergarten through grade 8, you might apply your deeper understanding as you present material related to the three focal points that *Curriculum Focal Points* identifies for instruction at your students' level. Or if you are teaching students in grades 9–12, you might use your understanding to enrich the ways in which you can engage students in mathematical reasoning and sense making as presented in *Focus in High School Mathematics: Reasoning and Sense Making*.

An enriched understanding can give you a fresh perspective and infuse new energy into your teaching. We hope that the understanding that you acquire from reading the book will support your efforts as you help your students grasp the ideas that will ensure their mathematical success.

The authors of the present volume wish to thank all of their reviewers, whose insightful comments caused them to think more deeply about important mathematics. They are especially grateful for the contributions of Richard Askey, Joanne Rossi Becker, Sandy Blount, Helen M. Doerr, Gail Keith, and Louis Lim.

Introduction

This book focuses on ideas about functions. These are ideas that you need to understand thoroughly and be able to use flexibly to be highly effective in your teaching of mathematics in grades 9–12. The book discusses many mathematical ideas that are common in high school curricula, and it assumes that you have had a variety of mathematics experiences that have motivated you to delve into— and move beyond—the mathematics that you expect your students to learn.

The book is designed to engage you with these ideas, helping you to develop an understanding that will guide you in planning and implementing lessons and assessing your students' learning in ways that reflect the full complexity of functions. A deep, rich understanding of these relationships will enable you to communicate their influence and scope to your students, showing them how these ideas permeate the mathematics that they have encountered—and will continue to encounter—throughout their school mathematics experiences.

The understanding of functions that you gain from this focused study thus supports the vision of *Principles and Standards for School Mathematics* (NCTM 2000): "Imagine a classroom, a school, or a school district where all students have access to high-quality, engaging mathematics instruction" (p. 3). This vision depends on classroom teachers who "are continually growing as professionals" (p. 3) and routinely engage their students in meaningful experiences that help them learn mathematics with understanding.

Why Functions?

Like the topics of all the volumes in NCTM's Essential Understanding Series, functions compose a major area of school mathematics that is crucial for students to learn but challenging for teachers to teach. Students in grades 9–12 need to understand functions well if they are to succeed in courses that build on quantitative thinking and relationships. Learners often have a narrow view of functions. On the basis of their frequent use of linear and quadratic functions, students tend to limit the concept of functions to equations or orderly rules. They frequently overlook many-to-one correspondences or irregular functions that could be very useful in describing or representing real-world phenomena. The importance of understanding functions and the challenge of understanding them well make them essential for teachers of mathematics in grades 9–12 to understand extremely well themselves.

Your work as a high school teacher of mathematics calls for a solid understanding of the mathematics that you—and your school, your district, and your state curriculum—expect your students to learn about functions. Your work also requires you to know how this mathematics relates to other mathematical ideas that your students will encounter in the lesson at hand, the current school year, and beyond. Rich mathematical understanding guides teachers' decisions in much of their work, such as choosing tasks for a lesson, posing questions, selecting materials, ordering topics and ideas over time, assessing the quality of students' work, and devising ways to challenge and support their thinking.

Understanding Functions

Teachers teach mathematics because they want others to understand it in ways that will contribute to success and satisfaction in school, work, and life. Helping your high school students develop a robust and lasting understanding of functions requires that you understand this mathematics deeply. But what does this mean?

It is easy to think that understanding an area of mathematics, such as functions, means knowing certain facts, being able to solve particular types of problems, and mastering relevant vocabulary. For example, as a teacher at the secondary level, you are expected to know facts such as "functions are single-valued mappings from one set to another" and "linear functions have a constant rate of change." It is likely that you need to be able to solve problems that involve tasks such as graphing a function or evaluating a function at a specific value. Your mathematical vocabulary is assumed to include such terms as *slope*, *maximum*, *minimum*, and *continuity*.

Obviously, facts, vocabulary, and techniques for solving certain types of problems are not all that you are expected to know about functions. In your ongoing work with students, you have undoubtedly discovered that you need to distinguish among different types of problems and know when particular strategies apply. For example, you must know the difference between linear and quadratic functions and the advantages and limitations of algebraic, tabular, and graphic representations of a function. You are also expected to be able to sort functions into families with common properties and describe the rate of change for particular functions.

It is also easy to focus on a very long list of mathematical ideas that all teachers of mathematics in grades 9–12 are expected to know and teach about functions. Curriculum developers often devise and publish such lists. However important the individual items might be, these lists cannot capture the essence of a rich understanding of the topic. Understanding this area deeply requires you not only to know important mathematical ideas but also to recognize how these ideas relate to one another. Your understanding continues to grow with experience and as a result of opportunities to embrace new ideas and find new connections among familiar ones.

Furthermore, your understanding of functions should transcend the content intended for your students. Some of the differences between what you need to know and what you expect them to learn are easy to point out. For instance, you need to understand rate of change in a way that connects with proportional reasoning in middle school as well as more advanced problems that analyze the rate of change in differential and integral calculus at the college level.

Other differences between the understanding that you need to have and the understanding that you expect your students to acquire are less obvious, but your experiences in the classroom have undoubtedly made you aware of them at some level. For example, how many times have you been grateful to have an understanding of functions that enables you to recognize the merit in a student's unanticipated mathematical question or claim? How many other times have you wondered whether you could be missing such an opportunity or failing to use it to full advantage because of a gap in your knowledge?

As you have almost certainly discovered, knowing and being able to do familiar mathematics are not enough when you're in the classroom. You also need to be able to identify and justify or refute novel claims. These claims and justifications might draw on ideas or techniques that are beyond the mathematical experiences of your students and current curricular expectations for them. Consider, for example, a claim that the popular technique of using a vertical line test to determine functionality is not applicable to all functions or the idea that sequences are functions.

Big Ideas and Essential Understandings

Thinking about the many particular ideas that are part of a rich understanding of functions can be an overwhelming task. Articulating all of those mathematical ideas and their connections would require many books. To choose which ideas to include in this book, the authors considered a critical question: What is *essential* for teachers of mathematics in grades 9–12 to know about functions to be effective in the classroom? To answer this question, the authors drew on a variety of resources, including personal experiences, the expertise of colleagues in mathematics and mathematics education, and the reactions of reviewers and professional development providers, as well as ideas from curricular materials and research on mathematics learning and teaching.

As a result, the mathematical content of this book focuses on essential knowledge for teachers about functions. In particular, chapter 1 is organized by five big ideas related to this important area of mathematics. Each of these big ideas is supported by smaller, more specific mathematical ideas, which the book calls *essential understandings*. This book focuses on three to seven interconnected essential understandings that are related to each big idea. These ideas elaborate what you need to know for an understanding of functions. Gaining this understanding is an extremely valuable and useful accomplishment because functions help us to think quantitatively about real-world phenomena. They provide us with ways to think about relationships—particularly change within those relationships.

Benefits for Teaching, Learning, and Assessing

An understanding of functions can help you implement the Teaching Principle enunciated in *Principles and Standards for School Mathematics*. This Principle sets a high standard for instruction: "Effective mathematics teaching requires understanding what students know and need to learn and then challenging and supporting them to learn it well" (NCTM 2000, p. 16). As in teaching about other critical topics in mathematics, teaching about functions requires knowledge that goes "beyond what most teachers experience in standard preservice mathematics courses" (p. 17).

Chapter 1 comes into play at this point, offering an overview of functions that is intended to be more focused and comprehensive than many discussions of the topic that you are likely to have encountered. This chapter enumerates, expands on, and gives examples of the big ideas and essential understandings related to functions, with the goal of supplementing or reinforcing your understanding. Thus, chapter 1 aims to prepare you to implement the Teaching Principle fully as you provide the support and challenge that your students need for robust learning about functions.

Consolidating your understanding in this way also prepares you to implement the Learning Principle outlined in *Principles and Standards*: "Students must learn mathematics with understanding, actively building new knowledge from experience and prior knowledge" (NCTM 2000, p. 20). To support your efforts to help your students learn about functions in this way, chapter 2 builds on the understanding of functions that chapter 1 communicates by pointing out specific ways in which the big ideas and essential understandings connect with mathematics that students typically encounter earlier or later in school. This chapter supports the Learning Principle by emphasizing longitudinal connections in students' learning about functions.

For example, foundations for ideas of function begin to develop in elementary school, where students study patterns and develop an informal notion of variable. By middle school, they are learning to represent patterns in tables and to look at covariation. In high school, students analyze these relationships and construct families of functions by studying characteristics of specific functions. In college, they extend their acquaintance with the domains of functions to include complex numbers, which may expand their notions about family characteristics.

The understanding that chapters 1 and 2 convey can strengthen another critical area of teaching. Chapter 3 addresses this area, building on the first two chapters to show how an understanding of functions can help you select and develop appropriate tasks, techniques, and tools for assessing your students' understanding of the topic. An ownership of the big ideas and essential understandings related to functions, reinforced by an awareness of students' past and future experiences with the ideas, can help you ensure that assessment in your classroom supports the learning of significant mathematics.

Such assessment satisfies the first requirement of the Assessment Principle set out in *Principles and Standards* (NCTM 2000): "Assessment should support the learning of important mathematics and furnish useful information to both teachers and students" (p. 22). An understanding of functions can also help you satisfy the second requirement of the Assessment Principle, by enabling you to develop assessment tasks that give you specific information about what your students are thinking and what they understand. For instance, you could ask a student to create (or select) equations that represent a given set of related graphs. This reversal of the common "graph this equation" assessment item can help you assess several of the essential understandings related to multiple big ideas of functions with one item.

Ready to Begin

This introduction has painted the background, preparing you for the big ideas and associated essential understandings related to functions that you will encounter and explore in chapter 1. Reading the chapters in the order in which they appear can be a very useful way to approach the book. Read chapter 1 in more than one sitting, allowing time for reflection. Absorb the ideas—both big ideas and essential understandings—that contribute to an understanding of functions. Appreciate the connections among these ideas. Carry your newfound or reinforced understanding to chapter 2, which guides you in seeing how the ideas related to functions are connected to the mathematics that your students have encountered earlier or will encounter later in school. Then read about teaching, learning, and assessment issues in chapter 3.

Alternatively, you may want to take a look at chapter 3 before engaging with the mathematical ideas in chapters 1 and 2. Having the challenges of teaching, learning, and assessment issues clearly in mind, along with possible approaches to them, can give you a different perspective on the material in the earlier chapters.

No matter how you read the book, let it serve as a tool to expand your understanding, application, and enjoyment of functions.

Functions: The Big Ideas and Essential Understandings

Because of their relevance to so many other mathematical topics and their role in college-level mathematics, functions constitute one of the most important topics in secondary school mathematics. They provide a means for thinking quantitatively about real-world phenomena and a context for studying relationships and change. Several "big ideas" permeate the teaching and learning of functions. We emphasize five of these ideas in this book.

Big Idea 1. The function concept. The concept of function is intentionally broad and flexible, allowing it to apply to a wide range of situations. The notion of function encompasses many types of mathematical entities in addition to "classical" functions that describe quantities that vary continuously. For example, matrices and arithmetic and geometric sequences can be viewed as functions.

Big Idea 2. Covariation and rate of change. Functions provide a means to describe how related quantities vary together. We can classify, predict, and characterize various kinds of relationships by attending to the rate at which one quantity varies with respect to the other.

Big Idea 3. Families of functions. Functions can be classified into different families of functions, each with its own unique characteristics. Different families can be used to model different real-world phenomena.

Big Idea 4. Combining and transforming functions. Functions can be combined by adding, subtracting, multiplying, dividing, and composing them. Functions sometimes have inverses. Functions can often be analyzed by viewing them as made from other functions.

Big Idea 5. Multiple representations of functions.

Functions can be represented in multiple ways, including algebraic (symbolic), graphical, verbal, and tabular representations. Links among these different representations are important to studying relationships and change.

Embedded in these big ideas are "essential understandings" that can provide foci for studying functions. Each of these essential understandings should be explicitly addressed in the teaching and learning of functions. We highlight those that we deem significant for students to learn. Each of these will be addressed in later sections. The list below numbers the essential understandings according to the big ideas with which this book most closely associates them, although they often apply to other big ideas as well.

Big Idea 1. The function concept

Essential Understanding 1a. Functions are single-valued mappings from one set—the *domain* of the function—to another—its *range*.

Essential Understanding 1b. Functions apply to a wide range of situations. They do not have to be described by any specific expressions or follow a regular pattern. They apply to cases other than those of "continuous variation." For example, sequences are functions.

Essential Understanding 1c. The domain and range of functions do not have to be numbers. For example, 2-by-2 matrices can be viewed as representing functions whose domain and range are a two-dimensional vector space.

Big Idea 2. Covariation and rate of change

Essential Understanding 2a. For functions that map real numbers to real numbers, certain patterns of covariation, or patterns in how two variables change together, indicate membership in a particular family of functions and determine the type of formula that the function has.

Essential Understanding 2b. A rate of change describes how one variable quantity changes with respect to another—in other words, a rate of change describes the covariation between two variables.

Essential Understanding 2c. A function's rate of change is one of the main characteristics that determine what kinds of real-world phenomena the function can model.

Big Idea 3. Families of functions

Essential Understanding 3a. Members of a family of functions share the same type of rate of change. This characteristic rate of change determines the kinds of real-world phenomena that the functions in the family can model.

Essential Understanding 3b. Linear functions are characterized by a constant rate of change. Reasoning about the similarity of "slope triangles" allows deducing that linear functions have a constant rate of change and a formula of the type $f(x) = mx + b$ for constants m and b.

Essential Understanding 3c. Quadratic functions are characterized by a linear rate of change, so the rate of change of the rate of change (the second derivative) of a quadratic function is constant. Reasoning about the vertex form of a quadratic allows deducing that the quadratic has a maximum or minimum value and that if the zeros of the quadratic are real, they are symmetric about the x-coordinate of the maximum or minimum point.

Essential Understanding 3d. Exponential functions are characterized by a rate of change that is proportional to the value of the function. It is a property of exponential functions that whenever the input is increased by 1 unit, the output is multiplied by a constant factor. Exponential functions connect multiplication to addition through the equation $a^{b+c} = (a^b)(a^c)$.

Essential Understanding 3e. Trigonometric functions are natural and fundamental examples of periodic functions. For angles between 0 and 90 degrees, the trigonometric functions can be defined as the ratios of side lengths in right triangles; these functions are well defined because the ratios of side lengths are equivalent in similar triangles. For general angles, the sine and cosine functions can be viewed as the y- and x-coordinates of points on circles or as the projection of circular motion onto the y- and x-axes.

Essential Understanding 3f. Arithmetic sequences can be thought of as linear functions whose domains are the positive integers.

Essential Understanding 3g. Geometric sequences can be thought of as exponential functions whose domains are the positive integers.

Big Idea 4. Combining and transforming functions

Essential Understanding 4*a*. Functions that have the same domain and that map to the real numbers can be added, subtracted, multiplied, or divided (which may change the domain).

Essential Understanding 4*b*. Under appropriate conditions, functions can be composed.

Essential Understanding 4*c*. For functions that map the real numbers to the real numbers, composing a function with "shifting" or "scaling" functions changes the formula and graph of the function in readily predictable ways.

Essential Understanding 4*d*. Under appropriate conditions, functions have inverses. The logarithmic functions are the inverses of the exponential functions. The square root function is the inverse of the squaring function.

Big Idea 5. Multiple representations of functions

Essential Understanding 5*a*. Functions can be represented in various ways, including through algebraic means (e.g., equations), graphs, word descriptions, and tables.

Essential Understanding 5*b*. Changing the way that a function is represented (e.g., algebraically, with a graph, in words, or with a table) does not change the function, although different representations highlight different characteristics, and some may show only part of the function.

Essential Understanding 5*c*. Some representations of a function may be more useful than others, depending on the context.

Essential Understanding 5*d*. Links between algebraic and graphical representations of functions are especially important in studying relationships and change.

Because the function concept is broad and flexible, it applies to every strand within the high school curriculum, from algebra to geometry and measurement to probability and data analysis. Thus, the study of functions can provide an organizational structure for the high school curriculum. However, because functions form such a large and important topic, the authors of a book of this size cannot hope to examine functions comprehensively. We therefore discuss only selected highlights in the study of functions at the high school level. We view functions from a particular perspective, focusing on the fact that a rate of change governs not only the kind of formula that a function has but also the kinds of situations that the function models. In this way, we use the perspective of calculus to examine functions that students study before they take calculus.

The Function Concept

Big Idea 1. *The concept of function is intentionally broad and flexible, allowing it to apply to a wide range of situations. The notion of function encompasses many types of mathematical entities in addition to "classical" functions that describe quantities that vary continuously. For example, matrices and arithmetic and geometric sequences can be viewed as functions.*

What are functions? This section discusses ways in which the concept of *function* can be defined and provides a sample of the range of situations in high school mathematics to which functions apply.

Originally, the notion of function arose to permit studying relationships between varying quantities in the physical world. For example, if an object is dropped from the top of a building, how is the height of the object above the ground related to the time that has elapsed since the object was dropped? How is the amount of time that a pendulum takes to complete a full swing back and forth related to the length of the pendulum? How is the area of a circular animal pen that is enclosed by a fence related to the length of the fence? Functions provide a framework for answering such questions.

Functions can show relationships between varying quantities

To study general relationships between two physical quantities such as height (or length), elapsed time, or area, it is useful to think of the quantities as varying over a range of possible values. For example, if an object is dropped from a height of 30 meters, the height of the object above the ground, in meters, ranges over the interval from 0 to 30. Every number between 0 and 30 occurs as the height of the object in meters at some time after the object was dropped. A useful insight in the development of functions was to let a letter, which we often call a variable, stand for a varying quantity. In a sense, by using a *variable,* we are able to work simultaneously with all the values that the quantity can attain. So equations that relate variables show relationships between many values all at once. Consider the problem in Reflect 1.1.

Reflect 1.1

Think about all possible circular animal pens enclosed by a length of fencing. For each length of fencing, there is the corresponding area that the fencing will enclose when it is formed into a circle. Describe the relationship between the area of a circular animal pen and the length of fencing that it takes to enclose the pen.

To show how the lengths of fencing and the areas of the animal pens are related, you may have written an equation equivalent to $A = \frac{L^2}{4\pi}$, or perhaps you wrote an equation equivalent to $L = 2\sqrt{\pi A}$, where L stands for the length of fencing and A stands for the area of the enclosed circular animal pen. You could also have made a table showing some possible lengths and corresponding areas. Perhaps you even sketched a graph. How are these ways of showing relationships between varying quantities related to the specific way that the concept of function is defined?

Definitions of *function*

Function is defined in many ways. Consider the selection of informal and formal definitions of *function* from middle school, high school, and college-level mathematics textbooks in table 1.1.

Table 1.1
Textbook definitions of *function*

A	A function is a relationship between input and output. In a function, the output depends on the input. There is exactly one output for each input.
B	A function is a relation in which each element of the domain is paired with *exactly* one element of the range.
C	A function is a set of ordered pairs (or number pairs) that satisfies this condition: There are no two ordered pairs with the same input and different outputs.
D	A real-valued function f defined on a set D of real numbers is a rule that assigns to each number x in D exactly one real number, denoted by f (x).
E	A function is a rule that assigns to each element of a set A a unique element of a set B (where B may or may not equal A).
F	For any sets A and B, a function f from A to B, f: A $\rightarrow$ B, is a subset f of the Cartesian product $A \times B$ such that every $a \in A$ appears once and only once as the first element of an ordered pair (a, b) in f.
G	A function is a mapping or correspondence between one set called the domain and a second set called the range such that for every member of the domain there corresponds exactly one member in the range.
H	One quantity, H, is a function of another, t, if each value of t has a unique value of H associated with it. We say H is the *value* of the function or the *dependent variable*, and t is the *argument* or *independent variable*. Alternatively, think of t as the *input* and H as the *output*.

Sources: Definitions A and B, Holliday et al. (2005), pp. 43 and 226, respectively.
Definition C, Interactive Mathematics Program (2000), p. 5.
Definition D, Edwards and Penney (2002), p. 2.
Definitions E and F, Usiskin et al. (2003), pp. 68 and 70.
Definition G, Saxon (2003), p. 152.
Definition H, Hughes-Hallet et al. (1994), p. 2.
Note: Italics as in originals; definition D defines *real-valued* functions only.

After reviewing the definitions in the table, think about the questions in Reflect 1.2. Consider them either by yourself or with a group of fellow teachers.

Reflect 1.2

Sort the function definitions into categories. (Photocopying the table and cutting the definitions into strips might be helpful.)

Write down the features of different definitions that led you to place them in the same group. Do your best to describe each group of definitions so that the distinctions among the groups become clearer.

After creating one set of groups, try to create another set by using different criteria.

On the basis of your work, consider (or discuss, if you are working with others) the following questions about the definitions in the table:

• What characteristics do the definitions of function seem to have in common? What differences appear?

• To what aspects of the function concept do *all* of the definitions draw students' and teachers' attention?

Notice that some of the definitions present functions as taking elements of one set to another set. These definitions present a function as taking inputs to outputs (consider definitions A and H), as a rule taking x to $f(x)$ (consider definitions D and E), or as a mapping, correspondence, or association from one set to another (consider definitions G and H). Other definitions present functions as sets of ordered pairs such that no two pairs have the same first entry but different second entries (consider definitions B, C, and F).

Recall the case of the circular animal pens enclosed by lengths of fencing in Reflect 1.1. Reflect 1.3 asks you to reconsider this case in light of the different definitions of *function* in table 1.1.

See Reflect 1.3 on p. 15.

When we associate to a length of fencing, L, the area of the circular pen it encloses, A, where A is related to L by the equation $A = \frac{L^2}{4\pi}$, then we are using a "mapping" view of function. By contrast, to use an "ordered pair" definition of function, we consider the ordered pairs of the form (L, A), where L and A are numbers such that $A = \frac{L^2}{4\pi}$. In both cases, L can run over all positive real numbers (allowing for reasonable lengths of the fence), since negative lengths of fencing do not make sense.

Note that when we describe a function by an equation of the form $y = f(x)$, we imply that a value for x is mapped to the value for y that makes the equation true. Yet, when we sketch a graph for

> **Reflect 1.3**
>
> Consider again the example of the circular animal pens enclosed by lengths of fencing.
>
> a. Use a "mapping" definition of *function*, viewing functions as taking one set to another, as in definition A, D, E, G, or H, to describe a function that arises from the situation of the circular animal pens.
>
> b. Use an "ordered pair" definition of *function*, viewing functions as certain sets of ordered pairs, as in definition B, C, or F, to describe a function that arises from the situation of the circular animal pens.
>
> c. Explain how the two types of definitions of *function* (as "mappings" [A, D, E, G, H] and as "ordered pairs" [B, C, F]) are related.

a function, we view the function as consisting of ordered pairs. In some sense, tables for functions bridge the "mapping" and "ordered pair" definitions of function because we can think of entries in the left-hand column of a table as mapping to the corresponding entries in the right-hand column, and we can also see the two entries in each row as an ordered pair.

"Single-valuedness" and the vertical line test

By definition, functions are "single-valued" (Essential Understanding 1*a*). In other words, for each element of the domain, there is exactly one element of the range of the function.

Single-valuedness is a central component of the treatment of function in many high school mathematics textbooks. Often, textbooks introduce the definition of function after a discussion of relations between sets. For example, definition B in table 1.1 portrays a function as a special type of relation—namely, a relation that is single-valued. Typically, in these textbooks, the definition of function is followed by a series of exercises in which students are asked to determine whether or not various relations are functions. Consider the tasks in Reflect 1.4, for example.

The relation depicted in Reflect 1.4 violates the single-valuedness requirement for functions because the input 0 is mapped to more than one output (both –2 and 1). In terms of ordered pairs, we can say that this relation is not a function from input to output, because 0 is the first element of more than one ordered pair: (0, –2) and (0, 1). Although a puddle diagram allows us to "see" that this mapping from a finite set of inputs to a finite set of outputs is not a function, there are many relationships that puddle diagrams cannot

Essential
Understanding 1a

Functions are single-valued mappings from one set—the domain *of the function—to another—its* range.

See Reflect 1.4 on p. 16.

Reflect 1.4

Mathematics textbooks often use "puddle diagrams" (or "mapping diagrams") such as the following to depict relations:

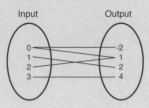

a. Use definition A or H to think about whether this mapping is a function from input to output.

b. Now use a different definition—one that does not contain the words *input* and *output*—to decide whether this mapping is a function.

c. What do puddle diagrams offer—or not offer—as representations of functions from input to output?

adequately depict or help us to classify. For example, we cannot adequately depict a function in which the domain is infinite by using a puddle diagram.

Before reading further, consider Reflect 1.5, which presents additional examples that highlight the single-valuedness of functions, as described in Essential Understanding 1*a*.

See Reflect 1.5 on p. 17.

→ → →

The relationship in part (*a*) is defined over a split domain. When $x < 2$, the relationship is constant: for each $x < 2$, the corresponding y-value is 3. Because each x corresponds to exactly one y-value (namely, 3), this piece of the relationship is single-valued. For many students, so-called *constant functions* are confusing because these relations do not seem single-valued (every x is mapped to the same constant), nor does the output seem to depend on the input. The other piece of the relationship in part (*a*) is also single-valued and is a linear function. Therefore, this piecewise-defined relationship is a function.

For parts (*b*) and (*c*) of Reflect 1.5, students would be likely to apply the so-called "vertical line test" to the graphs and determine that y is not a function of x. The vertical line test is often used to draw students' attention to the graphical representation of single-valuedness. Students can use this test to determine whether y is a function of x, given a graph of a relation, as follows:

> If every *vertical line* drawn goes through only one point of the graph, then y is a function of x. If a vertical line can be drawn that goes through two or more points, then y is not a function of x.

⇨ Essential Understanding 1*a*

Functions are single-valued mappings from one set—the domain of the function—to another—its range.

Reflect 1.5

In which of the following examples is *y* a function of *x*?

a. $y = 3$ if $x < 2$;
   $y = 2x - 2$ if $x \geq 2$

b. The set of all points on
   the graph shown below.

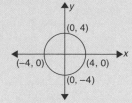

c. The set of all points on the
   graph shown below.

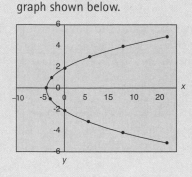

d.

x	y
−2	4
−1	1
0	0
1	1
2	4
3	9
4	16

Some teachers and researchers have suggested that a focus on the vertical line test can contribute to a tendency among students to apply rules mechanically rather than reasoning about the concept of function, particularly across different representations (e.g., Fernandez 2005). Understanding the concept of single-valuedness independently of graphical representations would help students to recognize that the relationships shown in parts (*a*) and (*d*) of Reflect 1.5 are single-valued and are functions.

Another criticism of the popular vertical line test is that it applies only when we associate to a graph the relation consisting of the ordered pairs of *Cartesian coordinates* (i.e., the usual *x*- and *y*-coordinates) of points on the graph. But given a graph, if we view the points in terms of *polar coordinates*, then the set of ordered pairs formed in this way can be a function even if the relation obtained from the Cartesian coordinates is not. For example, the circle shown in part (*b*) of Reflect 1.5, when viewed in terms of polar coordinates where the angle is listed first, consists of all ordered pairs of the form $(\theta, 4)$, and this relation *is* a function. (The typical notation for polar coordinates is (r, θ); however, we reversed the order so that the ordered pairs would be a function.) As illustrated in the graph in figure 1.1, this circle includes points such as (45°, 4) and (165°, 4).

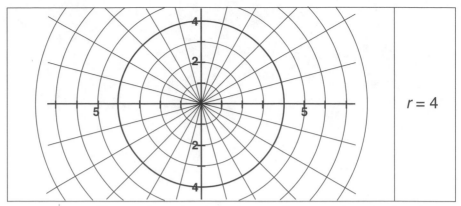

Fig. 1.1. A graph using polar coordinates to show the function
consisting of ordered pairs (θ, r) where θ is the angle measured
counterclockwise from the positive x-axis and r = 4

In part (c) of Reflect 1.5, although y is not a function of x, the graph does represent a functional relationship: x is a function of y. To some extent, the vertical line test may deter students from exploring these important aspects of graphical representations.

High school textbooks have placed considerable emphasis on the idea of single-valuedness—particularly through exercises in which students distinguish between relations and functions. However, single-valuedness is primarily a "technical" requirement that makes functions more manageable and less ambiguous to work with (Freudenthal 1983). For example, the square root function is defined so that $sqrt(x)$ equals the nonnegative y satisfying $y^2 = x$. Otherwise, each x would correspond to two y values (e.g., 4 would correspond to ±2), and we would need to specify which value we were talking about at a given time. An important application of square roots is finding distances between two points. For instance, the distance between the points (0, 0) and (x, y) is $sqrt(x^2 + y^2)$. Negative answers would not make sense, so it is convenient that the square root function is defined to be nonnegative. Considerations such as these led mathematicians to restrict functions to those that are single-valued.

The concept of function is broad and flexible

In high school, the study of function centers on classical functions whose domain and range consist of intervals within the real numbers and which are given by well-known formulas. At the heart of the study of functions in high school lie linear functions, quadratic functions, polynomial functions in general, some of the inverses of these functions, such as square and cube roots, as well as exponential functions and their inverses, the logarithmic functions, trigonometric functions, and rational functions. However, other functions arise in high school mathematics as well. Some of these functions are not defined by a single simple formula, such as step functions and other functions that are defined piecewise. Some functions, such as sequences, are different from the classical functions because they are defined on discrete sets (integers) rather than on intervals and thus do not have the kind of "continuous variation" that the classical functions do. Other functions have domains or ranges that do not lie within the real numbers. For example, the area function for rectangles depends on two variable quantities—namely, the length and the width of the rectangle. As stated in Essential Understanding 1*b*, the function concept is broad enough to encompass these and many other nonclassical examples.

Functions without single formulas

Functions do not have to be defined by formulas. For example, the function that takes the number of days since a seedling was planted to the seedling's height in centimeters is a function that generally is not described by a formula (although within a range, the function may be approximated by a formula).

Some functions are defined piecewise, with different formulas applying to different parts of the domain, such as the example in part (*a*) of Reflect 1.5. Although functions that are defined piecewise may seem strange, we encounter them in daily life. The amount of postage that a letter requires, when viewed as a function of the weight of the letter, is a step function.

Although the absolute value function is given by a simple formula, namely, $y = |x|$, we can also view this function as defined piecewise:

$$y = x \quad \text{if} \quad x \geq 0$$
$$y = -x \quad \text{if} \quad x < 0$$

Students often do not recognize this function as the absolute value function, because it appears to have negative values. Examples such as $-(-3) = 3$ can help students see why the function defined piecewise above is in fact the absolute value function.

Sequences as nontraditional functions

A sequence is a list of items (usually numbers) in order, such as 5, 9, 13, 17, 21, ..., or 1, 1/2, 1/4, 1/8, 1/16, 1/32, ..., or a sequence of patterns, such as the sequence of dot patterns in figure 1.2. Although we do not often think of them this way, sequences are in fact functions (Essential Understanding 1*b*)—namely, functions whose domains are the positive integers (or sometimes the nonnegative integers, if we wish to have a "0th entry"). Let *N*

Essential Understanding 1*b*

Functions apply to a wide range of situations. They do not have to be described by any specific expressions or follow a regular pattern. They apply to cases other than those of "continuous variation." For example, sequences are functions.

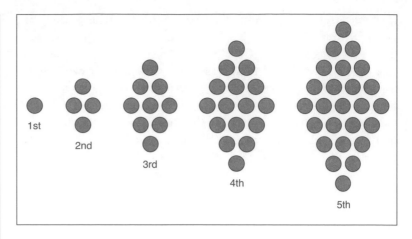

Fig. 1.2. A growing sequence of dot patterns

denote the positive integers. For a sequence, a_1, a_2, a_3, ... (where the a_n are real numbers), the corresponding function, $f : N \to R$, is defined by $f(n) = a_n$. Viewing sequences in this way allows seeing many sequences as coming from functions whose domains are all real numbers simply by restricting the domain to the positive integers. For example, the sequence 5, 9, 13, 17, ... can be viewed as the restriction to the positive integers of the function f given by $f(x) = 4x + 1$ because $f(1) = 5$, $f(2) = 9$, $f(3) = 13$, and so on.

Because we can always restrict a function that is defined on all the real numbers to just the positive integers and thus obtain a sequence, analyzing a sequence can be a first step toward analyzing a function whose domain is all real numbers. As we will see later, arithmetic sequences are restrictions of linear functions to the positive integers, and geometric sequences are restrictions of exponential functions to the positive integers. But most important, the reasoning that we employ in analyzing sequences is often a simplified version of the reasoning that we use to analyze the corresponding functions that are defined on the full set of real numbers. Thus, analyzing sequences can be a good starting point for analyzing certain functions.

Parametric equations

The points in the plane that satisfy the equation $x^2 + y^2 = 1$ form a unit circle, but the equation for the circle describes a relation for which y is not a function of x. Nevertheless, there are functions that map the real numbers to the unit circle. One such function sends a real number, θ, to the point $(\cos(\theta), \sin(\theta))$. Although the domain of this function is the real numbers, its range does not lie within the real numbers but is instead the unit circle in the plane (Essential

➡ Essential
Understanding 1c

The domain and range of functions do not have to be numbers. For example, 2-by-2 matrices can be viewed as representing functions whose domain and range are a two-dimensional vector space.

Understanding 1c). We can think of this function as wrapping the real number line around the unit circle infinitely many times. In this way, a single variable serves as a parameter for the circle, or in other words, the real line "parameterizes" the circle.

Another way to parameterize the unit circle produces Pythagorean triples. Consider all nonvertical lines in the plane that go through the point (–1, 0). Each such line meets the circle in a point other than (–1, 0). We can therefore define a function from the real numbers to the unit circle by sending a real number t to this point on the circle that the line of slope t through (–1, 0) meets. Reflect 1.6 invites exploration of this situation.

Reflect 1.6

Consider the point (x, y) where the line with slope t through the point (–1, 0) meets the unit circle (other than the point (–1, 0)). Write equations that describe the x- and y-coordinates of this point as functions of t.

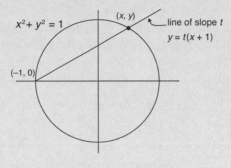

The x- and y-coordinates of the point under consideration in Reflect 1.6 are given by

$$x = \frac{1 - t^2}{1 + t^2} \text{ and } y = \frac{2t}{1 + t^2}.$$

To obtain these formulas, we can substitute $y = t(x + 1)$ in $x^2 + y^2 = 1$. Then we can view $x^2 + t^2(x + 1)^2 = 1$ as a quadratic equation in x with coefficients in t and apply the quadratic formula to solve for x in terms of t. Notice that these coordinates are closely related to Pythagorean triples: if we let t run over the positive integers and let $a = t^2 - 1$, $b = 2t$, and $c = 1 + t^2$, then $a^2 + b^2 = c^2$, and a, b, and c form Pythagorean triples. If we let t run over all positive rational numbers p/q, where p and q are relatively prime positive integers, and use $p^2 - q^2$, $2pq$, and $p^2 + q^2$ for a, b, and c, respectively, we actually get all primitive Pythagorean triples. (See Silverman [1997] for further discussion of Pythagorean triples and the unit circle.)

→ Essential
Understanding 1c

*The domain and
range of functions
do not have to be
numbers. For
example, 2-by-2
matrices can be
viewed as represent-
ing functions whose
domain and range
are a two-
dimensional vector
space.*

Isometries as functions

Isometries of the plane—namely, translations, rotations, reflections, and glide reflections—are functions that map the plane to the plane. These functions are important in geometry but are not defined on the real numbers (Essential Understanding 1c). In fact, from an advanced mathematical perspective, the "distance preserving functions" on a space are what define the geometry of the space. More generally, mathematicians often study the functions on a space as a means to study the space itself.

Matrices as functions

Matrices represent an important family of functions that are not defined on the real numbers (Essential Understanding 1c). A major purpose of matrices is to solve systems of linear equations. To understand the theory of solving systems of linear equations, viewing matrices as representing functions is helpful.

To view 2-by-2 matrices as representing functions from the plane to the plane, we can let R^2 denote Euclidean 2-space (the plane)—namely, the set of all vectors (v_1, v_2), where v_1 and v_2 are real numbers. We can view Euclidean 2-space either as row vectors, as just defined, or as column vectors—namely, as all vectors of the form $\begin{pmatrix} v_1 \\ v_2 \end{pmatrix}$, where v_1 and v_2 are real numbers—choosing whichever is more appropriate for the circumstance. We can view a 2–by-2 matrix $A = \begin{pmatrix} a_{11} & a_{12} \\ a_{21} & a_{22} \end{pmatrix}$, whose entries are real numbers, as a function whose domain and range are both R^2, which we indicate by writing $A : R^2 \to R^2$. That is, the matrix A takes the input vector $v = \begin{pmatrix} v_1 \\ v_2 \end{pmatrix}$ in R^2 to the output vector

$$A_v = \begin{pmatrix} a_{11} & a_{12} \\ a_{21} & a_{22} \end{pmatrix} \begin{pmatrix} v_1 \\ v_2 \end{pmatrix} = \begin{pmatrix} a_{11}v_1 + a_{12}v_2 \\ a_{21}v_1 + a_{22}v_2 \end{pmatrix}$$

in R^2. In this way, a 2-by-2 matrix can be viewed as representing a function from the plane to the plane.

We have provided only a few examples of the many different kinds of functions that arise throughout mathematics other than those functions that map real numbers to real numbers.

Covariation and Rate of Change

Big Idea 2. *Functions provide a means to describe how related quantities vary together. We can classify, predict, and characterize various kinds of relationships by attending to the rate at which one quantity varies with respect to the other.*

One of the main uses of functions that map real numbers to real numbers is to model real-world situations in which one quantity changes in relation to another quantity. For example, the distance that a falling object has traveled depends on the time that has elapsed since the object was dropped. To describe and analyze functions, it is often useful to recognize them as members of particular families of functions (Essential Understanding 2*a*).

Furthermore, to recognize a function as a member of a family, we often attend to the way in which the output of a function changes as the input changes. When we attend to how changes in input produce changes in output, we are attending to *covariation*. The rate of change of a function—namely, the rate at which the output of the function changes in relation to a change in the input—is a way to quantify the idea of covariation (Essential Understanding 2*b*).

Essential Understanding 2*a*

For functions that map real numbers to real numbers, certain patterns of covariation, or patterns in how two variables change together, indicate membership in a particular family of functions and determine the type of formula that the function has.

Covariation

When you look at a table for a function, what stands out most, and what is easiest to observe? Examine the table of the function f in figure 1.3. What do you notice? What stands out?

x	$f(x)$
−1	1
0	1
1	3
2	7
3	13
4	21

Fig. 1.3. A table of values for the function $f(x)$

Essential Understanding 2*b*

A rate of change describes how one variable quantity changes with respect to another—in other words, a rate of change describes the covariation between two variables.

The most readily observable feature in a table for a function is often the way in which the two columns change. When we focus on the way in which two varying quantities change together, we are taking a *covariation perspective*. From a covariation perspective, "a function is understood as the juxtaposition of two sequences, each of which is generated independently through a pattern of data values" (Confrey and Smith 1995, p. 67). When we take a covariation perspective, we generally don't focus on rules relating x and $f(x)$; instead, we examine "the coordination of two data columns" (p. 78)—in other words, how changes in one variable relate to changes in another variable. Question (a) in Reflect 1.7 probes this perspective.

Reflect 1.7

a. What would be involved in examining the relationship represented in part (d) of Reflect 1.5 from a covariation perspective? (For the reader's convenience, the table from Reflect 1.5 part (d) is repeated below.)

x	y
−2	4
−1	1
0	0
1	1
2	4
3	9
4	16

b. What would be involved in examining the same relationship from a *correspondence perspective*?

A covariation perspective focuses on patterns in how two variables change together. For example, the relationship represented in the table for part (d) of Reflect 1.5 (reproduced above in Reflect 1.7) can be examined by noticing the changing quantities in the two columns of the table. One might observe that as x increases by 1, y increases by a nonconstant amount. The specific pattern of covariation exhibited by the function in Reflect 1.5 part (d) is characteristic of quadratic functions, as is explored in detail later in this book.

Question (b) in Reflect 1.7 explores a different perspective. In contrast to a covariation perspective, a *correspondence view* of function draws attention to a mapping from one set to another. From this perspective, the relationship in Reflect 1.5 part (d) can be viewed as the mapping from x to y: −2 → 4, −1 → 1, 0 → 0, etc. This correspondence can also be represented $y = x^2$.

In recent years, a consensus has been growing for the view that a covariation approach furnishes an important first step in the direction of a fuller comprehension of the function concept. The Standards of the National Council of Teachers of Mathematics (NCTM 1989, 2000) emphasize functions as covariation or dependence relationships.

The notion of emphasizing function as covariation is consistent with research indicating that when students examine problems involving functional situations, they typically use a covariation perspective before attempting to generalize the relationships (Confrey and Smith 1994, 1995). As Smith (2003) has argued, "Beginning with a covariational approach can provide the basis for developing a correspondence relationship that can then be expressed algebraically" (p. 145). For example, by "coordinating" the values in the two columns of data in the table in figure 1.4 (i.e., looking for patterns in the columns simultaneously), students can use a covariation approach to describe the rate of change in this function (Confrey and Smith 1995). By recognizing that $f(x)$ increases by 5 for each unit change in x, students are prepared to develop an algebraic equation to describe the linear relationship between x and $f(x)$.

x	$f(x)$
−2	−10
0	0
2	10
4	20
6	30
8	40

Fig. 1.4. By "coordinating" the data in the two columns to determine the rate of change, students use a covariation approach.

A covariation view of function may support later understanding of mathematics. Some researchers, investigating college students' understanding of function, have suggested that such a view of function is essential for understanding key ideas of calculus and for interpreting and reasoning about average and instantaneous rates of change in real-world situations (Carlson and Oehrtman 2005).

Rate of change

The notion of *rate of change* of a function provides a mechanism to describe and quantify the covariation between two variables.

Average and instantaneous rates of change

What is rate of change? Let's start with an example. Suppose that it starts to rain at noon. Let's say that between 2 PM and 6 PM a total of 12 millimeters of rain falls. At every time between noon and 6 PM (at least), a certain total amount of rain has fallen (measured from the time when the rain started to fall). Therefore, we can consider a "rainfall function" whose inputs are times in hours since the rain started falling (so these inputs are between 0 and 6, at least), and whose corresponding outputs are the total amount of rain that has fallen at that time. We can ask, "At what rate is the rain falling?" or, posing the question another way, "What is the rate of change of the rainfall function?" Consider the questions in Reflect 1.8.

Reflect 1.8

What is the average rate of change of the rainfall function between 2 PM and 6 PM?

What, if anything, does this rate tell us about the amount of rain that fell between 2 PM and 3 PM, between 3 PM and 4 PM, between 4 PM and 5 PM, and between 5 PM and 6 PM?

Because 12 millimeters of rain fell over a span of 4 hours, when we consider the amount of rain that fell over the 4 hour-long intervals from 2 PM to 3 PM, from 3 PM to 4 PM, from 4 PM to 5 PM, and from 5 PM to 6 PM, the average of these amounts is 3 millimeters. This does not mean that 3 millimeters of rain fell each hour—more rain might have fallen at first, and then the rain might have tapered off—but the average of the amounts of rain that fell in those hour-long intervals was 3 millimeters. So, we can say that the average rate of change of the rainfall function between 2 PM and 6 PM is 3 millimeters per hour. We found this average rate of change of the rainfall function by dividing the 12-millimeter change in the rainfall function between 2 PM and 6 PM by the length of the time interval over which this change occurred, or 4 hours.

In the same way, given any (real-valued) function f defined on an interval $[a, b]$, we say that the *average rate of change* of this function over the interval is the change in the value of the function from a to b divided by the length of the interval from a to b. (To simplify the language, this book will often use only "rate of change" instead of "average rate of change.") Because the change in the value of the function between a and b is $f(b) - f(a)$, and the length of the interval from a to b is $b - a$, the average rate of change of f over the interval $[a, b]$ is

$$\frac{f(b) - f(a)}{b - a}.$$

Another way to describe the average rate of change is as the change in outputs divided by the change in inputs. In a graphical setting, we often describe this change in outputs divided by change in inputs as "rise over run," which is the slope of the line through $(a, f(a))$ and $(b, f(b))$; see figure 1.5.

The study of the relationship between a function and its rates of change is the heart of calculus. In calculus, we work with

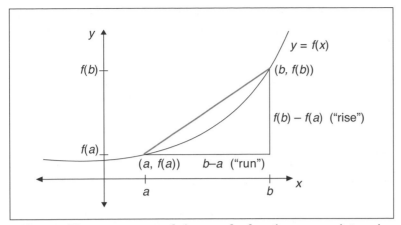

Fig. 1.5. The average rate of change of a function over an interval

instantaneous rates of change, which we obtain from average rates of change by allowing the intervals to become smaller and smaller. For example, if we let *b* move closer and closer to *a*, so that the point (*b*, *f*(*b*)) slides down the curve, closer and closer to point (*a*, *f*(*a*)), as shown in figure 1.6, the average rate of change will get closer and closer to the instantaneous rate of change. The instantaneous rate of change of *f* at the input *a* is called the *derivative* of *f* at *a*. In terms of the graph of *f*, the derivative is the slope of the *tangent line* to *f* at *a*, which, speaking informally, is the line that just "grazes" the graph and goes in the same direction as the graph at (*a*, *f*(*a*)). As *b* moves closer and closer to *a*, so that (*b*, *f*(*b*)) moves closer and closer to (*a*, *f*(*a*)), the slope of the line between (*a*, *f*(*a*)) and (*b*, *f*(*b*)) becomes closer and closer to the slope of the tangent line at (*a*, *f*(*a*)), as indicated by the colored lines in the figure. In the case of the rainfall function in Reflect 1.8, the instantaneous rate of change of the rainfall function tells us the rate at which the rain is falling at a given moment in time.

Rate of change versus change

As we have seen, the rates of change of a function are rates, not differences. If students are used to working only with tables in

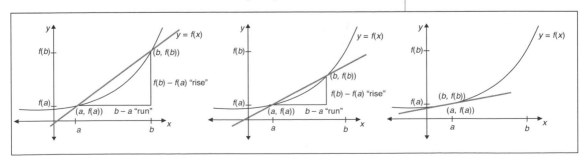

Fig. 1.6. The instantaneous rate of change of a function at a point

which the inputs increase by 1 unit, they may focus only on *change* in the outputs, and not on *rates of change*. To emphasize the distinction between changes in the output values of functions and rate of change, teachers can create situations in which students' attention to change or rate of change has implications for their interpretations of the situation. For instance, consider the questions in Reflect 1.9.

Reflect 1.9

A park ranger measured the depth of the water in a lake at the same spot over a period of several weeks and recorded the results in a table:

Day	Depth of the lake in meters
7	15.29
14	15.43
28	15.57
35	15.71
42	15.85

a. What was the change in depth from day 7 to day 14?

b. What was the change in depth from day 14 to day 28?

c. What was the average rate of change in depth from day 7 to day 14? From day 14 to day 28? From day 7 to day 42?

In the scenario in Reflect 1.9, the change in depth of the lake from day 7 to day 14 is 0.14 meters, and the change in depth from day 14 to day 28 is 0.14 meters. However, the average rate of change from day 7 to day 14 is 0.02 meters per day, and the average rate of change from day 14 to day 28 is 0.01 meters per day. The rates of change are different because the periods of time are different (7 days as opposed to 14 days). Students who focus only on changes in the "depth of the lake" column of the table, without considering changes in the "day" column, are unlikely to recognize the different rates of change. Although all the *differences* in the "depth of the lake" column are 0.14 meters, the rate of change is not constant. Experience with such problems will help students develop the concept in Essential Understanding 2*b*.

➡ Essential Understanding 2*b*

A rate of change describes how one variable quantity changes with respect to another—in other words, a rate of change describes the covariation between two variables.

Rates of change and formulas

A function's rate of change is one of the main characteristics that determine what kinds of real-world situations the function models (Essential Understanding 2*c*). The rate of change is also one of the main characteristics that determine the nature of a formula for the function and its membership in a family of functions, as we will see next in the case of arithmetic sequences and geometric sequences, as well as later in the case of other functions, thus illustrating Essential Understanding 2a. In the case of arithmetic and geometric sequences, we can see especially clearly how we can start with a covariation view, in which we focus on change, and from there, derive a formula for the function, which describes a correspondence between variables.

Arithmetic sequences: Deducing formulas from rates of change

The sequence 5, 9, 13, 17, 21, ..., in which each term is 4 more than the previous term, is an arithmetic sequence; so is the sequence 1.6, 1.1, 0.6, 0.1, –0.4, –0.9, –1.4, ..., in which each term is 0.5 less than the previous term. In general, a sequence is called *arithmetic* if there is a constant m (which can be positive, negative, or zero) such that each term in the sequence (beyond the first term) can be obtained from the previous term by adding m. We can describe the arithmetic sequence as obtained by the recursive rule NEXT = NOW + m. This recursive rule tells us how the entries in the sequence change as we go from one entry ("NOW") to the next. Described differently, if the Nth entry of the arithmetic sequence is denoted $A(N)$, then $A(N + 1) = A(N) + m$. Viewed from a function perspective, the recursive rule tells us how the outputs change as the inputs increase by 1.

When we write the first few entries in an arithmetic sequence, such as 1, 4, 7, 10, 13, ... , it is the way in which the entries in the sequence change from one to the next that is most apparent and most useful for finding the next few entries. But what if we want to know the 100th entry? In this case, we will want to know a formula for the sequence. In other words, we will want a formula for the Nth entry in terms of N, or, expressed in yet another way, we will want to know a formula that tells us how an entry depends on its position in the sequence. Although it can often be easy to guess the formula for an arithmetic sequence, there is a systematic way to find the formula and to explain why it is valid. We will see later that this reasoning is a simpler version of the reasoning that explains why linear functions all have formulas of the familiar $mx + b$ form. Reflect 1.10 focuses on two simple arithmetic sequences.

← ← ←

You probably noticed that the amount by which an arithmetic sequence changes from one entry to the next (in other words, the m in NEXT = NOW + m) is the coefficient of N in a formula for the Nth entry of the sequence. We can explain why this must be the case. To understand this important line of reasoning, let's work with an example. Consider the arithmetic sequence 3, 7, 11, 15, ..., which

Essential ←
Understanding 2c

A function's rate of change is one of the main characteristics that determine what kinds of real-world phenomena the function can model.

Essential ←
Understanding 2a

For functions that map real numbers to real numbers, certain patterns of covariation, or patterns in how two variables change together, indicate membership in a particular family of functions and determine the type of formula that the function has.

See Reflect 1.10 on p. 30.

Reflect 1.10

Describe the recursive rules for the arithmetic sequences 1, 4, 7, 10, 13, ... and 1, 5, 9, 13, 17, ...

Find formulas in terms of N for the Nth entries of the sequences (you may guess the formulas).

What relationship do you see between the recursive rules and the formulas? Try to explain why the formulas must be valid for all entries.

increases by 4 as we go from one entry to the next, so that the recursive rule for the sequence is NEXT = NOW + 4. The first entry of the sequence is 3, its second entry is 4 more than 3, which is 7, its third entry is 4 more than 7, which is 11, and so on. If the sequence had a 0th entry, what would it be? It would be –1 because when we add 4, we get 3, which is the first entry. Now think about obtaining each entry in the sequence by starting from the 0th entry; see figure 1.7. (Note that although we could also start with the 1st entry, we start with the 0th entry because of the especially nice connection with formulas for linear functions.) Observe the pattern:

To get the first entry, start at –1 and add 4 one time.

To get the second entry, start at –1 and add 4 two times.

To get the third entry, start at –1 and add 4 three times.

In general, to get the Nth entry, start at –1 and add 4 N times.

Therefore the Nth entry is –1 + 4N, or 4N – 1.

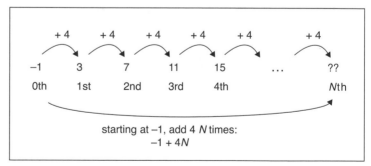

Fig. 1.7. Using the way that an arithmetic sequence changes to derive a formula

In general, the reasoning in the previous paragraph shows that if an arithmetic sequence changes according to the recursive rule NEXT = NOW + m, and if the 0th entry is b (which is obtained from the first entry by subtracting m), then the Nth entry of the sequence is given by the formula $mN + b$. Conversely, if there are constants m and b such that the Nth entry of a sequence is given by the formula $mN + b$, so that the sequence is $m + b$, $2m + b$, $3m + b$, $4m + b$, ..., then the sequence changes by adding m as one goes from one entry to the next and is therefore an arithmetic sequence.

To summarize, we can say that arithmetic sequences form a family of functions whose domains are the positive integers. The way in which an arithmetic sequence changes from one entry to the next plays a major role in a formula $mN + b$ that describes how the Nth entry depends on N, illustrating Essential Understanding 2a. Notice that if we substitute x for N in the formula $mN + b$, and if we allow x to take on all real numbers as values (rather than just counting numbers), we get the familiar $mx + b$ formula for linear functions (Essential Understanding 3f). We will see later why all linear functions must take this form.

Geometric sequences: Deducing formulas from rates of change

Geometric sequences are the multiplicative counterpart of arithmetic sequences. The sequence 2, 6, 18, 54, ..., where each entry is 3 times the previous entry, is a geometric sequence, and so is the sequence 5, 5/2, 5/4, 5/8, ..., where each entry is 1/2 times the previous entry. In general, a sequence is called *geometric* if there is a positive constant b such that each term in the sequence (beyond the first term) can be obtained from the previous term by multiplying by b. We can describe the geometric sequence as obtained by the recursive rule NEXT = NOW · b, which tells us how the function changes as we go from one entry to the next. Viewed from a function perspective, the recursive rule tells us how the outputs change as the inputs increase by 1.

Like arithmetic sequences, geometric sequences form a family of functions, all of which have the same type of formula. The formula for a geometric sequence is determined in large part by the way in which a geometric sequence changes, and we can explain why formulas for geometric sequences take the form that they do. Consider the sequences in Reflect 1.11.

Essential Understanding 2a

For functions that map real numbers to real numbers, certain patterns of covariation, or patterns in how two variables change together, indicate membership in a particular family of functions and determine the type of formula that the function has.

Essential Understanding 3f

Arithmetic sequences can be thought of as linear functions whose domains are the positive integers.

Reflect 1.11

Describe the recursive rules for the geometric sequences 10, 20, 40, 80, ... and 5, 5/3, 5/9, 5/27, ...

Find formulas in terms of N for the Nth entries of the sequences (you may guess the formulas initially).

What relationship do you see between the recursive rules and the formulas? Try to explain why the formulas must be valid for all entries.

Let's consider the geometric sequence 7, 7/2, 7/4, 7/8, ... Each entry (beyond the first) is 1/2 times the previous entry. If the sequence had a 0th entry, it would be 14, because 1/2 times 14 is the first entry, 7. Let's think about how we can get each entry by starting from the 0th entry, 14 (see fig. 1.8). Observe the pattern:

To get the first entry, we multiply the 0th entry by 1/2 one time, obtaining $14 \cdot \left(\frac{1}{2}\right)$.

To get the second entry, we multiply the 0th entry by 1/2 two times, obtaining $14 \cdot \left(\frac{1}{2}\right)^2$.

To get the third entry, we multiply the 0th entry by 1/2 three times, obtaining $14 \cdot \left(\frac{1}{2}\right)^3$.

In general, to get the Nth entry, we multiply the 0th entry by 1/2 N times, obtaining $14 \cdot \left(\frac{1}{2}\right)^N$, as indicated in the figure.

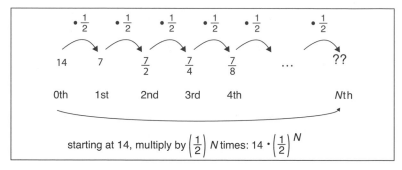

Fig. 1.8. Using the way that a geometric sequence changes to derive a formula

The reasoning in the previous paragraph shows that if a geometric sequence changes according to the recursive rule NEXT = NOW · b, and if the 0th entry is A (which is obtained from the first entry by dividing by b), then the Nth entry of the sequence is given by the formula $A \cdot b^N$. Conversely, if there are constants A and b such that the Nth entry of a sequence is given by the formula $A \cdot b^N$, then the sequence is $A \cdot b$, $A \cdot b^2$, $A \cdot b^3$, ..., where each entry is b times the previous entry, and the sequence is therefore a geometric sequence.

To summarize, we can say that geometric sequences form a family of functions whose domains are the counting numbers. Geometric sequences are characterized by multiplying (or dividing) by a fixed amount as one goes from one entry to the next. In other words, geometric sequences are characterized by a recursive rule of the form NEXT = NOW · b for some positive constant b (which can be less than 1). The constant b in the recursive rule is a key component in the formula $A \cdot b^N$ for the Nth entry of a geometric sequence. In particular, the way in which the sequence changes plays a major role in a formula that describes how the Nth entry depends on N, thus illustrating Essential Understanding 2*a*. Notice that if we replace N with x in the formula $A \cdot b^N$, and if we allow x to take on all real numbers as values (rather than just counting numbers), we get, by definition, the exponential functions (Essential Understanding 3*g*)—which are characterized by formulas of the form $A \cdot b^x$, where A and b are constants (with A not zero and b positive).

A technical note: In the case of arithmetic sequences, the number m in the recursive rule NEXT = NOW + m is the rate of change of the sequence. In the case of geometric sequences, however, the number b in the recursive rule NEXT = NOW $\cdot$ b is not the actual rate of change of the sequence, even though it tells us how the sequence changes and describes the sequence from the perspective of covariation. In the case of geometric sequences, the actual rates of change are not constant.

Essential ← Understanding 2*a*

For functions that map real numbers to real numbers, certain patterns of covariation, or patterns in how two variables change together, indicate membership in a particular family of functions and determine the type of formula that the function has.

Essential ← Understanding 3*g*

Geometric sequences can be thought of as exponential functions whose domains are the positive integers.

Families of Functions and Their Role in Modeling Real–World Phenomena

Big Idea 3. *Functions can be classified into different families of functions, each with its own unique characteristics. Different families can be used to model different real-world phenomena.*

A cornerstone of high school (and college) mathematics is the study of various families of functions, including polynomial functions, rational functions, exponential functions, logarithmic functions, and trigonometric functions. Within these families are subfamilies, and even families within the subfamilies. For example, within the polynomial functions, the quadratic functions and linear functions are especially important. Within the linear functions, the direct proportions (which have equations of the form $y = mx$) form a subfamily. The most obvious way in which the functions within a family fit together is that their formulas are similar. For example, every linear function has a formula of the form $f(x) = mx + b$ for some constants m and b. However, the functions within a family are generally related in more important ways, such as through the specific properties that they share and therefore also through the kinds of situations that they model. Often, these properties, as well as the kinds of real-world situations that the functions model, are related to the ways in which the outputs of the functions change as the inputs change (i.e., the *covariation* or *rate of change*), thus illustrating Essential Understandings 2*c* and 3*a*. Consider the rates of change of the functions in Reflect 1.12. To what families do these functions belong?

→ → →

The six relationships represented in Reflect 1.12 belong to three families of functions that are common elements of the high school mathematics curriculum: linear, quadratic, and exponential. Parts (*c*) and (*d*) represent linear functions, parts (*a*) and (*f*) represent quadratic functions, and parts (*b*) and (*e*) represent exponential functions. Each of these examples and types of functions are discussed in this section. Classification into these families of functions, as well as other function families common to the high school curriculum (such as logarithmic functions and trigonometric functions, which are periodic), has the main purpose of drawing attention to the nature of change in different situations—particularly those that occur in real-world contexts. Familiarity with prototypical patterns of change can help in constructing and interpreting different representations of functions in various problem contexts. For instance, knowledge of a variety of different types of function rules and

→ Essential Understanding 2c

A function's rate of change is one of the main characteristics that determine what kinds of real-world phenomena the function can model.

See Reflect 1.12 on p. 35.

→ Essential Understanding 3a

Members of a family of functions share the same type of rate of change. This characteristic rate of change determines the kinds of real-world phenomena that the functions in the family can model.

Reflect 1.12

For each of the following functions, make a table of some values (if such a table is not given), plot some points on the graph of the function (if a graph is not given), and use both the table and the graph to discuss the *rate of change* of each function.

To what major family of functions does each relationship belong? How did you decide?

a. The function that associates to the input *x* the output *y* given by $y = 5x^2 + 3$.

b. The 2010 Census shows that Smallville has a population of 40,000 people. Social scientists predict that Smallville will experience a growth rate of 5% per year over the next 20 years. Let *P* be the function such that *P*(*t*) is the predicted population of Smallville *t* years from now (for *t* between 0 and 20).

c. A movie theater has operating costs of $1025 per day. Tickets cost $7.50 each. The theater's profit each day depends on the number of tickets sold. Let *P* be the function such that *P*(*T*) is the profit that the movie theater will make on a day when it sells *T* tickets.

d. The function whose input-output table is shown below:

D	M
7	15.29
14	15.43
21	15.57
28	15.71
35	15.85

e. The function whose graph is shown below:

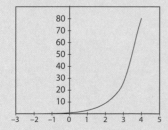

f. Fred is deciding which size of pizza is the best buy. He wonders how the area of the pizza is related to its diameter. Let *A* be the function such that *A*(*r*) is the area of a circular pizza of radius *r*.

graphs can be very helpful for finding models for patterns in data and understanding the behavior of those patterns. Perhaps most important, the patterns of different families of functions offer organizational tools for describing mathematical change.

Linear functions

Typically, the first function family to which students are introduced is *linear functions*. By definition, a function is called *linear* if its graph lies on a straight line. Reflect 1.13 focuses on this geometric definition.

Linear functions are characterized by a constant rate of change

Suppose that we have a linear function f. By definition, this means that the graph of $y = f(x)$ lies on a line. What can we say about the rate of change of such a function? The key to answering this question is the similar "slope triangles" that are created from a horizontal "run" segment, a vertical "rise" segment, and a segment of the graph itself. The triangles ABC and DEF in figure 1.9 are examples of slope triangles.

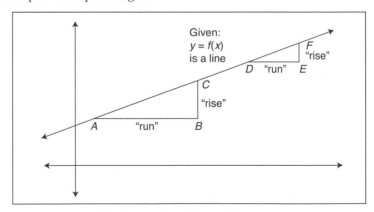

Fig. 1.9. Slope triangles of a linear function

Triangles ABC and DEF are similar because they have congruent angles, and these angles are congruent because they are created when parallel lines intersect the graph. Specifically, the angles at A and D are congruent because both are created when horizontal, and thus parallel, lines meet the graph of the function. The angles at B and E are congruent because both are right angles formed from horizontal and vertical lines. The remaining angles at C and F must therefore also be congruent (since the sum of the interior angles in a triangle is 180 degrees). Because ABC and DEF have congruent angles, these triangles are similar, so the ratios "rise"/"run" are equal in both triangles. Because "rise"/"run" is another way to say "change in output"/"change in input," which is a rate of change of the function, this rate of change is therefore constant for a linear function, and this insight is Essential Understanding 3b. The constant ratio "rise"/"run" is what we call the *slope* of the line; it is a measure of the line's steepness. Students should be aware that even though we use the term "rise," the "rise" is negative when the line slopes downward.

We can also reverse the above line of reasoning to explain why functions that have a constant rate of change are linear. Given a function that has a constant rate of change, all the slope triangles created by the segment joining two points on the graph of the function and the corresponding horizontal "run" segment and vertical "rise" segment must be similar because they are right triangles whose corresponding side lengths have the same ratios. Because all the slope triangles are similar, all the corresponding angles of these triangles are congruent, and so the graph must lie on a line. So, if a function has a constant rate of change, its graph lies on a line, and hence the function is linear. We have thus established that linear functions are characterized by a constant rate of change, which is part of Essential Understanding 3b.

Essential ← Understanding 3b

Linear functions are characterized by a constant rate of change. Reasoning about the similarity of "slope triangles" allows deducing that linear functions have a constant rate of change and a formula of the type f(x) = mx + b for constants m and b.

Linear functions have formulas of the form $f(x) = mx + b$

We have defined linear functions geometrically, as functions whose graphs lie on a line. Why does such a function necessarily have a formula of the familiar type $f(x) = mx + b$? Again, the key to answering this question is the rate of change, which we can examine once again by working with slope triangles. Starting with a given function $f(x)$ whose graph lies on a line, let's consider why there are constants m and b such that $f(x) = mx + b$. Let $b = f(0)$—namely, the y-intercept. (Let's assume that 0 is in the domain of f. Otherwise, we can pick any other number that is in the domain, and the argument works in the same way.) Let m be the slope of the line, which is the constant "rise"/"run" ratio that is created by any slope triangle. If (x, y) is a point on the line (but not on the y-axis), then $(0, b)$, (x, b), and (x, y) are the vertices of a slope triangle (as seen in fig .10), and using this triangle, we see that the slope is $\frac{y-b}{x}$. Because the slope is always equal to the constant m, $\frac{y-b}{x} = m$. Solving for y, we see

*For functions that
map real numbers to
real numbers, certain
patterns of covaria-
tion, or patterns in
how two variables
change together,
indicate membership
in a particular fam-
ily of functions and
determine the type
of formula that the
function has.*

that $y = mx + b$. Because $y = f(x)$, we can also say that $f(x) = mx + b$, which is what we wanted to show. Notice that the constant rate of change of a linear function determines the type of formula that a linear function has, illustrating Essential Understanding 2a.

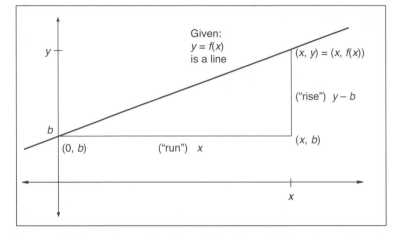

Fig. 1.10. Using a slope triangle to find a formula for a linear function

Conversely, if a function f is given by a formula of the form $f(x) = mx + b$, where m and b are constants, what can we say about the rate of change of the function? If we put in any two values for x in the domain of f—say, r and s—then the rate of change of f from r to s is

$$\frac{f(s) - f(r)}{s - r} = \frac{(ms + b) - (mr + b)}{s - r} = \frac{m(s - r)}{s - r} = m,$$

so the function has a constant rate of change, and therefore its graph lies on a line. Reflect 1.14 probes connections between linear functions, with formulas of the type $mx + b$, and arithmetic sequences, with formulas of the type $mN + b$.

Reflect 1.14

Compare the reasoning that we used to explain why linear functions have a formula of the form $mx + b$ and the reasoning that we used previously to explain why arithmetic sequences have formulas of the form $mN + b$.

If you view an arithmetic sequence as a function and graph it, what does the graph look like?

Equivalent descriptions of linear functions

The previous paragraphs prove that the following are equivalent for a function f whose domain and range lie within the real numbers:

- The graph of f lies on a line

- All the slope triangles on the graph are similar

- The rate of change of f is constant
- There are constants m and b such that $f(x) = mx + b$ for all x in the domain of f (the constant m is the constant rate of change of f).

The reasoning that we used to connect these equivalent characterizations of linear functions is a key part of Essential Understanding 3*b* and shows that the algebraic and graphical representations of linear functions are deeply connected (Essential Understanding 5*d*).

Linear functions modeling real-world situations

Linear functions have constant rates of change and describe many real-world situations, including the following:

- The cost of buying a certain number of equally priced items (cost as a function of the number of items)
- Income earned in working for a fixed hourly wage (income as a function of the number of hours worked)
- A bathtub or swimming pool filling with water from a steady stream (volume as a function of elapsed time)
- The progress of a student walking to school at a steady pace (distance as a function of elapsed time)

These examples illustrate Essential Understandings 3*a* and 3*b*. To be modeled by a linear function, each of these situations must involve a rate that remains *constant*: equally priced items (price per item is constant), a fixed hourly wage (wages earned per hour worked is constant), a steady stream of water (volume of water per unit amount of time is constant), and a steady walking speed (distance walked per unit amount of time is constant). If a situation is modeled by a linear function, then the change in output divided by the change in input—the rate of change of the function—is constant. Conversely, if a situation involves a constant rate of change, then it is modeled by a linear function.

Let's consider in detail the situation in part (c) of Reflect 1.12. A movie theater sells tickets for $7.50 apiece and has operating costs of $1025 a day. For each ticket sold, the profit increases by a constant amount: $7.50. This constant rate of change of $7.50 per ticket sold can also be obtained from a table representing the situation, even when the table's input values increase by increments other than 1. Consider a table in which each entry for T is 50 greater than the previous entry, as in figure 1.11.

In the table, the differences between consecutive values for P are each $375. This change in P occurs each time T increases by 50. Therefore, the rate of change is $375/50 = $7.50 per ticket sold.

**Essential ←
Understanding 3*b***

Linear functions are characterized by a constant rate of change. Reasoning about the similarity of "slope triangles" allows deducing that linear functions have a constant rate of change and a formula of the type $f(x) = mx + b$ for constants m and b.

**Essential ←
Understanding 5*d***

Links between algebraic and graphical representations of functions are especially important in studying relationships and change.

**Essential ←
Understanding 3*a***

Members of a family of functions share the same type of rate of change. This characteristic rate of change determines the kinds of real-world phenomena that the functions in the family can model.

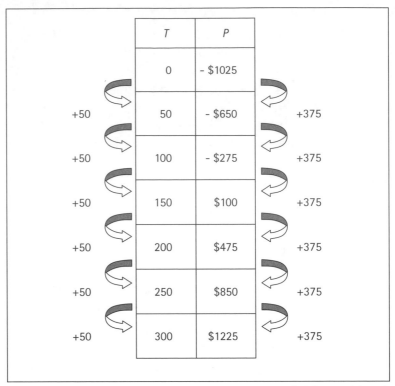

T	P
0	- $1025
50	- $650
100	- $275
150	$100
200	$475
250	$850
300	$1225

+50 ... +50 ... +50 ... +50 ... +50 ... +50

+375 ... +375 ... +375 ... +375 ... +375 ... +375

Fig. 1.11. A table of values showing *T*, the number of tickets sold, and *P*, the profit after daily operating costs, for a movie theater

Given the data in the table, we could have also found the rate of change without considering the differences between consecutive values for *P*, by selecting *any* two input-output pairs:

Rate of change = change in output / change in input
= (–650 – (–1025))/(50 – 0) = \$7.50 per ticket.

Two different input-output pairs will yield the same rate of change:

Rate of change = change in output / change in input
= (850 – 100)/(250 – 150) = \$7.50 per ticket.

If we represent the table shown in figure 1.11 in graphical form, can we see the rate of change? Consider the graph in figure 1.12.

Although the specific rate of change (\$7.50 per ticket sold) is not immediately visible in the graph, the linear nature of the graph and the constantly increasing profit in the table are apparent. By adjusting the scales on the axes of the graph, we can gain access to the rate of change, as figure 1.13 shows.

As we have seen, all linear functions can be expressed in the form $f(x) = mx + b$, where m is the constant rate of change (or *slope*) and b is the value of $f(0)$. The movie theater situation from Reflect 1.12 part (c) can be represented by the rule $P = 7.5T - 1025$, where *P* is the profit and *T* is the number of tickets sold. In this rule,

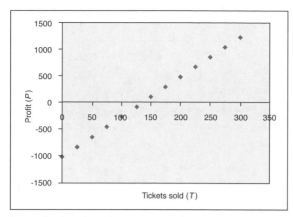

Fig. 1.12. A graph showing the constant change of the values in the table in figure 1.11

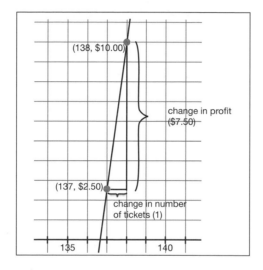

Fig. 1.13. Adjusting the scale of the graph in figure 1.12 to make the rate of change visible

the rate of change ($7.50 per ticket sold) plays an important role, as does the value –$1025, representing the profit when zero tickets have been sold (with the negative sign indicating that the "profit" is actually a loss). Consider the two functions and rates of change in Reflect 1.15.

← ← ←

As we have illustrated in this section, all linear functions have a constant rate of change that can be represented in several ways: (1) by the slope (the direction and steepness) of the graph, (2) by the constant increment of numerical change in the table values, and (3) by the coefficient of x in $f(x) = mx + b$. Thus, linear functions provide an example of a family of functions that is characterized by a distinct pattern of covariation, which is related to a distinct kind of formula (Essential Understanding 2a).

Essential Understanding 2a

For functions that map real numbers to real numbers, certain patterns of covariation, or patterns in how two variables change together, indicate membership in a particular family of functions and determine the type of formula that the function has.

stop
reflect

See Reflect 1.15 on p. 42.

Reflect 1.15

Use the strategies illustrated in the text to identify the rate of change in the situation represented in part (*d*) of Reflect 1.12. (The table of values is shown below for the reader's convenience.)

Table from Reflect 1.12, part (*d*)

D	M
7	15.29
14	15.43
21	15.57
28	15.71
35	15.85

Compare the rate of change of this function to the rate of change in the situation shown in Reflect 1.9. (Again, the table is shown below for the reader's convenience.)

Table from Reflect 1.9

Day	Depth of the lake in meters
7	15.29
14	15.43
28	15.57
35	15.71
42	15.85

Why is the function in Reflect 1.12 part (*d*) linear, but the function in Reflect 1.9 is nonlinear?

Linear versus nonlinear situations

Let's consider two situations that seem similar in some ways but are quite different when viewed from the perspective of linear functions.

Situation 1: Given that a temperature of 0 degrees Celsius is 32 degrees Fahrenheit and that a temperature of 100 degrees Celsius is 212 degrees Fahrenheit, how can we determine what a temperature measured in degrees Celsius, such as 25 degrees Celsius, is in degrees Fahrenheit?

Situation 2: An orange juice factory has many vats of the same size, which the factory fills with orange juice, and many hoses of the same size, through which orange juice flows at the same rate into the vats.

If it takes 5 minutes for 6 hoses to fill a vat, and it takes 3 minutes for 10 hoses to fill a vat, then how long will it take some other number of hoses, such as 8 hoses, to fill a vat?

Reflect 1.16 explores these situations.

Reflect 1.16

Answer the questions about situations 1 and 2. In each case, decide whether the situation can be modeled by a linear function, and explain why or why not.

If a linear function can model a situation, use it to answer the question. In each case, try to use reasoning that does not draw explicitly on functions.

In situation 1, let F be the function that assigns to a temperature C in degrees Celsius the corresponding temperature $F(C)$ in degrees Fahrenheit. Is F a linear function? Yes, because no matter what the temperature of an object is, if its temperature is raised by 1 degree Celsius, it will be raised by a constant number of degrees Fahrenheit. In other words, the rate of change of the function F is constant. Because $F(0) = 32$ and $F(100) = 212$, this constant rate of change is

$$\frac{212 - 32}{100 - 0} = \frac{9}{5}, \quad \text{so} \quad F(C) = \frac{9}{5}C + 32.$$

Therefore, a temperature of 25 degrees Celsius is $F(25)$, or 77 degrees Fahrenheit. Informally, we could also reason that since 25 degrees Celsius is 1/4 of the way between 0 degrees and 100 degrees Celsius, the temperature in degrees Fahrenheit must be 1/4 of the way between 32 and 212 degrees. Because 212 − 32 = 180 and 1/4 of 180 is 45, it follows that 25 degrees Celsius is 32 + 45, or 77 degrees Fahrenheit.

Situation 2 is different. Reasoning in the following way is tempting, but incorrect: 8 is halfway between 6 and 10. So, since 6 hoses take 5 minutes and 10 hoses take 3 minutes, the time that 8 hoses take should be halfway between 5 minutes and 3 minutes. We would conclude, incorrectly, that it should take 4 minutes for 8 hoses to fill a vat. Reflect 1.17 examines this reasoning.

Reflect 1.17

Why is the seemingly plausible reasoning detailed in the text about how long it should take to fill a vat with 8 hoses incorrect?

This reasoning about how long 8 hoses should take to fill the vat is incorrect because it treats the time that it takes to fill a vat as a linear function of the number of hoses used. If we let T be the function that assigns to a number of hoses, H, the number of minutes $T(H)$ that it takes to fill the vat by using that many hoses, then this function does not have a constant rate of change. Reflect 1.18 probes the situation.

Reflect 1.18

Use logical reasoning to fill in the entries in the table for the function $T(H)$. Then explain why this function does not have a constant rate of change.

H	T
3	
6	5
12	
24	

If 6 hoses take 5 minutes to fill a vat, then twice as many hoses, 12, should take half as long, or 2.5 minutes, to fill it. Similarly, since 6 hoses take 5 minutes to fill the vat, half as many hoses, 3, should take twice as long, or 10 minutes, to fill it. However, the average rate of change of the function T between $H = 3$ and $H = 6$ is not the same as the average rate of change of T between $H = 6$ and $H = 12$, so T is not a linear function. Thus, we cannot use the seemingly plausible reasoning by "linear interpolation" described above to find the time that 8 hoses take to fill a vat. Instead, we can reason that since 6 hoses take 5 minutes to fill the vat, 1 hose will take 6 times as long, or 30 minutes, and 8 hoses will take 1/8 as long as one hose to fill it. Thus, 8 hoses will take 3.75 minutes to fill the vat.

Another way to reason is to notice that the number of hoses, H, and the time, T, that it takes to fill the vat, are inversely proportional, because the product $H \cdot T$ must remain constant. This product must be constant because whenever we multiply the number of hoses by an amount, the time that it takes to fill the vat is divided by that amount. Thus, an equation relating H and T is $H \cdot T = 30$, so $T = \frac{30}{H}$, and we can use this formula to find the time that it takes to fill the vat by using any number of hoses. These examples indicate that the key to distinguishing linear from nonlinear situations is that linear functions are characterized by a constant rate of change. This is the idea in Essential Understanding 3b.

➡️ Essential Understanding 3b

Linear functions are characterized by a constant rate of change. Reasoning about the similarity of "slope triangles" allows deducing that linear functions have a constant rate of change and a formula of the type $f(x) = mx + b$ for constants m and b.

Quadratic functions

Students' first experiences with nonconstant rates of change often occur when they study situations modeled by *quadratic functions*. For quadratic functions (e.g., parts (*a*) and (*f*) of Reflect 1.12), the rate of change is not constant, but its rate of change is itself changing at a constant rate (Essential Understanding 3c).

By definition, quadratic functions are functions that can be written in the form $f(x) = ax^2 + bx + c$ for some constants *a*, *b*, and *c*, where *a* is not 0. Quadratic functions provide opportunities for students to reason mathematically and are important in basic physics, which explores questions such as those in Reflect 1.19.

Reflect 1.19

Do heavier objects fall faster than lighter ones, and is the speed at which an object falls proportional to its weight?

Does an object fall at a constant speed?

Before the time of Galileo (1564–1642), people generally believed that heavier objects fall faster than lighter ones, that the speed at which an object falls is constant, and that the speed of a falling object is proportional to the weight of the object. Of course, air resistance *does* cause a feather to fall to the ground more slowly than a marble, for example. But if we drop two objects that are shaped in such a way that they encounter minimal air resistance (if both are in the shape of a marble, say), they will both hit the ground at the same time, even if one is lighter than the other. Some science museums have exhibits featuring a feather and an iron ball, each in a vacuum tube, to show that both fall at the same (nonconstant) rate. Galileo determined that the speed at which an object falls to the ground is not constant but increases with time and that the distance an object falls is a quadratic function of the elapsed time.

Since the time of Newton (1643–1727), we have used calculus to explain why the height of a falling object is a quadratic function of elapsed time. This explanation is based on two facts: that the acceleration due to gravity is (approximately) constant near the surface of the earth, and that acceleration is the second derivative of the height function. It turns out that we can characterize quadratic functions as those functions whose second derivative—the rate of change of the rate of change—is a nonzero constant, illustrating Essential Understandings 3c and 2a. Furthermore, it is the characterization of quadratic functions in terms of rates of change that explains why the relationships between heights of falling objects and elapsed time are quadratic, which is an example of the idea in Essential Understanding 2c.

Essential ← Understanding 3c

Quadratic functions are characterized by a linear rate of change, so the rate of change of the rate of change (the second derivative) of a quadratic function is constant. Reasoning about the vertex form of a quadratic allows deducing that a quadratic has a maximum or minimum value and that if the zeros of the quadratic are real, they are symmetric about the x-coordinate of the maximum or minimum point.

Essential
Understanding 2c

A function's rate of change is one of the main characteristics that determine what kinds of real-world phenomena the function can model.

First and second differences of quadratic functions

Before we study quadratic functions in terms of first and second derivatives, which are instantaneous rates of change, we can get a sense of the derivatives by considering first and second differences, which are average rates of change. Figure 1.14 shows the average rate of change of the quadratic function $g(x) = x^2 + x + 1$ on the interval from 0 to 1, from 1 to 2, from 2 to 3, and so on. These are the "first differences" of $g(x)$, which approximate the derivative of $g(x)$.

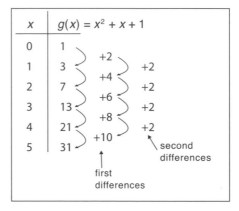

Fig. 1.14. First and second differences of a quadratic function

Essential
Understanding 3c

Quadratic functions are characterized by a linear rate of change, so the rate of change of the rate of change (the second derivative) of a quadratic function is constant. Reasoning about the vertex form of a quadratic allows deducing that a quadratic has a maximum or minimum value and that if the zeros of the quadratic are real, they are symmetric about the x-coordinate of the maximum or minimum point.

The figure also shows the "second differences" of $g(x)$—the "change in the change"—which approximate the second derivative of $g(x)$. Notice that the second differences are constant. In fact, a nonzero constant second difference is characteristic of quadratic functions.

Quadratic functions as heights of falling objects

When an object falls (without air resistance), it experiences a constant acceleration—namely, the acceleration due to gravity, which is −32 feet per second per second near the surface of the earth (it is negative because the acceleration is downward). If $h(t)$ is the height of an object above the ground in feet t seconds after the object is thrown up or down, or simply dropped, then the first derivative, $h'(t)$, is the velocity of the object after t seconds, and the second derivative, $h''(t)$, is the acceleration of the object after t seconds. So, we are given that $h''(t) = -32$. Because this second derivative is the constant function −32, the first derivative must be a function whose derivative is −32, and therefore the first derivative must be of the form $h'(t) = -32t + v$ for some constant v. Similarly, since the function $h(t)$ has derivative $-32t + v$, it must be of the form $h(t) = -16t^2 + vt + p$ for some constant p. The very same analysis shows that every function whose second derivative is a nonzero constant must be a quadratic function. You can quickly check that the second derivative of a quadratic function is a nonzero constant. Therefore, the quadratic functions are exactly those functions whose second derivative is a nonzero constant, illustrating Essential Understanding 3c.

As we have seen, it is physics, together with this characterization of quadratic functions, that explains why the heights of falling objects are quadratic functions of the time elapsed since the object was dropped or thrown. As in the case of linear functions, we see that the nature of a function's rate of change determines its membership in the family of quadratic functions and plays an important role in the real-world situations that it models, illustrating Essential Understandings 2a and 3a. Reflect 1.20 invites further examination of the formula $h(t) = -16t^2 + vt + p$ for the height of a falling object t seconds after it has been dropped or thrown.

Essential Understanding 2a

For functions that map real numbers to real numbers, certain patterns of covariation, or patterns in how two variables change together, indicate membership in a particular family of functions and determine the type of formula that the function has.

Reflect 1.20

Interpret the constants v and p in the formula $h(t) = -16t^2 + vt + p$ for the height of a falling object t seconds after it is dropped or thrown. Keep in mind that $h'(t) = -32t + v$ is the velocity of the falling object. What do v and p stand for in the situation?

Because the velocity of the object after t seconds is given by $h'(t) = -32t + v$, evaluating at $t = 0$ gives us $h'(0) = v$, so v is the velocity of the object at time 0. In other words, v is the initial velocity of the object. If the object is simply dropped, then v is 0, but if the object is thrown upwards, then v is a positive number that depends on how hard the object was thrown. What about p? Evaluating $h(t) = -16t^2 + vt + p$ at $t = 0$, we see that $h(0) = p$. Therefore, p is the position (height) of the object at time 0, or in other words, it is the initial height from which the object was dropped or thrown.

Our analysis has produced the height function as a quadratic in standard form. In this form, the initial height and initial velocity of the object appear as coefficients. Another familiar form for a quadratic function is *vertex form*. As we will see next, we can get other useful information about the height function from its vertex form.

Essential Understanding 3a

Members of a family of functions share the same type of rate of change. This characteristic rate of change determines the kinds of real-world phenomena that the functions in the family can model.

Quadratics in vertex form

The standard form for a quadratic function is $y = ax^2 + bx + c$, where a, b, and c are constants. But we often put quadratic functions in *vertex form*—that is, in the form $y = a(x - h)^2 + k$, where a, h, and k are constants. Reflect 1.21 explores the usefulness of this form.

Reflect 1.21

What is the purpose of putting a quadratic function in vertex form?

What information does the vertex form of a quadratic provide, and why?

→ Essential
Understanding 3c

*Quadratic functions
are characterized
by a linear rate of
change, so the rate
of change of the
rate of change (the
second derivative) of
a quadratic function
is constant. Reason-
ing about the vertex
form of a quadratic
allows deducing
that a quadratic
has a maximum or
minimum value and
that if the zeros
of the quadratic
are real, they are
symmetric about
the x-coordinate
of the maximum or
minimum point.*

Vertex form allows us to deduce that quadratic functions and their graphs have certain features (Essential Understanding 3c). Given a quadratic in vertex form, $y = a(x - h)^2 + k$, where a, h, and k are constants, we can deduce the following:

1. *a*. If $a > 0$, the quadratic has a minimum value, k, occurring at $x = h$.

   b. If $a < 0$, the quadratic has a maximum value, k, occurring at $x = h$, so the point (h, k) on the graph is either a minimum or maximum point and is called a *vertex*.

2. The zeros of the quadratic (i.e., the x-intercepts—namely, the x-values for which the function has value 0) occur at $x = h \pm \sqrt{\dfrac{-k}{a}}$; thus the quadratic has two zeros that are symmetrically placed around $x = h$ if $\dfrac{-k}{a} > 0$, one zero at $x = h$ if $k = 0$, and no real zeros if $\dfrac{-k}{a} < 0$.

The key to deducing fact 1 is noticing that since $(x - h)^2$ is a square, it will be greater than or equal to 0 no matter what value is substituted for x. So, for part (*a*) of fact 1, if $a > 0$, then the value of $a(x - h)^2$ is greater than or equal to 0 for all x, and thus the smallest value that the quadratic can attain is k, which occurs when $x - h = 0$. Using similar reasoning, we deduce part (*b*) of fact 1. Thus, the point (h, k) on the quadratic is a maximum point if $a < 0$ and is a minimum point if $a > 0$, as shown in figure 1.15; we call this point a *vertex*.

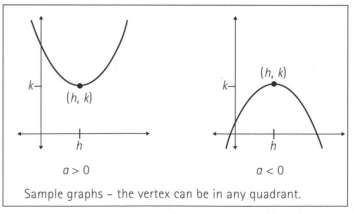

Sample graphs – the vertex can be in any quadrant.

Fig. 1.15. The vertex (h, k) on the graph of $y = a(x - h)^2 + k$

To deduce fact 2, we must solve the equation $a(x - h)^2 + k = 0$. An equation in this form is set up to be easy to solve by reducing it to an equation of the form "square = constant," which we can solve by taking a square root. Each of the following equations is equivalent—that is, each has the same set of solutions:

$$a(x - h)^2 + k = 0$$

$$(x - h)^2 = \frac{-k}{a}$$

$$x - h = \pm\sqrt{\frac{-k}{a}}$$

$$x = h \pm \sqrt{\frac{-k}{a}}$$

Thus, the zeros of a quadratic function occur symmetrically about the vertex, as depicted in figure 1.16.

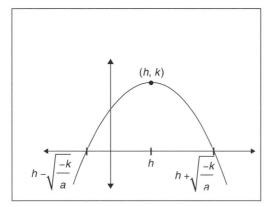

Fig. 1.16. The zeros (x-intercepts) of $y = a(x - h)^2 + k$ occur symmetrically about the vertex.

Applying standard and vertex forms to the height of a falling object

Consider the example of a projectile that is launched upward from an initial height of 144 feet above the ground with an initial (upward) velocity of 128 feet per second. If we assume that air resistance is negligible, then we can use our result from previous paragraphs (see pp. 46–47) to say that the height of the object above the ground t seconds after launch is $h(t) = -16t^2 + 128t + 144$ feet. Consider the questions in Reflect 1.22 about different forms of this equation.

← ← ←

See Reflect 1.22 on p. 50.

From the standard form for the height of the projectile, $h(t) = -16t^2 + 128t + 144$, we can readily see that the initial height of the projectile is 144 feet, since $h(0) = 144$. Also, from the previous discussion, we know that the initial velocity of the projectile is given by the coefficient of the linear term, 128 feet per second.

Reflect 1.22

What information about the projectile can we readily deduce from the standard form for its height, $h(t) = -16t^2 + 128t + 144$?

What information about the projectile can we readily deduce from the vertex form for its height, $h(t) = -16(t - 4)^2 + 400$?

➡️ Essential Understanding 3c

Quadratic functions are characterized by a linear rate of change, so the rate of change of the rate of change (the second derivative) of a quadratic function is constant. Reasoning about the vertex form of a quadratic allows deducing that a quadratic has a maximum or minimum value and that if the zeros of the quadratic are real, they are symmetric about the x-coordinate of the maximum or minimum point.

From the vertex form for the projectile's height, $h(t) = -16(t - 4)^2 + 400$, we deduce that the maximum height that the projectile reaches is 400 feet and that this occurs 4 seconds after launch. Notice that we can quickly reason why this is so, thus illustrating Essential Understanding 3c. The term $-16(t - 4)^2$ is always less than or equal to 0, because the square, $(t - 4)^2$, must always be greater than or equal to 0. Therefore, the largest value that $h(t)$ can ever have is 400, and this occurs when $t - 4$ is 0.

We can also use vertex form to determine when the projectile hits the ground. We know that the projectile hits the ground at a time t when $h(t) = 0$. So, we should solve $-16(t - 4)^2 + 400 = 0$ for t. We can apply the general formula for the roots of a quadratic in vertex form that we developed previously, or, better yet, we can reproduce the reasoning that led to the formula, thus producing the following equivalent equations:

$$-16(t - 4)^2 + 400 = 0,$$
$$400 = 16(t - 4)^2,$$
$$25 = (t - 4)^2,$$
$$\pm 5 = t - 4$$

So, the projectile hits the ground at $t = 9$ seconds or $t = -1$ seconds. In this case, $t = -1$ doesn't make sense (the projectile cannot hit the ground before it was launched), so we know that the projectile hits the ground 9 seconds after launch. We can see the symmetry about the x-coordinate of the vertex in the zeros of the quadratic function when we solve the quadratic equation in vertex form, again illustrating Essential Understanding 3c. Our analysis of the projectile wouldn't be complete without a graph; see Reflect 1.23.

Reflect 1.23

How can we use the information that we have obtained so far from the standard form and the vertex form of the projectile's height function to sketch a graph of this function?

We have found the following information about the height of the projectile t seconds after launch, as given by $h(t) = -16t^2 + 128t + 144 = -16(t - 4)^2 + 400$. At time $t = 0$, the projectile's height is 144 feet; at time $t = 4$ seconds, its height is 400 feet, and this is the maximum height attained. At time $t = 9$ seconds, the projectile hits the ground. These pieces of information yield the points (0, 144), (4, 400), and (9, 0), along with the knowledge that (4, 400) must be the highest point on the graph. Together, these pieces of information are enough to allow us to deduce that the graph must look at least roughly like the one in figure 1.17.

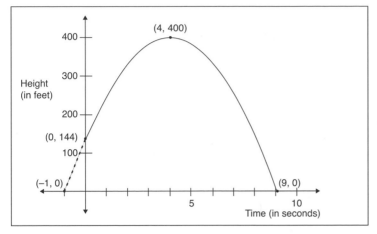

Fig. 1.17. Graph of a projectile's height function

Furthermore, if $h(t)$ were an abstract function rather than height as a function of time, the point (–1, 0) would also be on the graph, since we found that $t = -1$ was also a solution to $h(t) = 0$. Reflect 1.24 probes what the graph does or does not show in relation to the real-world situation of the projectile.

Reflect 1.24

Does the graph in figure 1.17 show us the path along which the projectile travels from launch to when it hits the ground? Why or why not?

Beware that when we graph the height of an object as a function of time, the graph *does not* necessarily show us the path along which the object travels. This is because the independent variable, or x-axis, is not horizontal location but elapsed *time*. In the example under discussion, the projectile was launched straight upward, so its path of motion is on a vertical line, and it has no horizontal motion.

Putting quadratics in vertex form and the quadratic formula

As we have seen, when a quadratic function is in vertex form, we can use a nice line of reasoning to find its zeros. So, to find roots of quadratic equations, it is useful to put the quadratic into vertex form. Reflect 1.25 explores the relationship between vertex form and the quadratic formula.

How is vertex form related to the quadratic formula?

→ Essential
Understanding 3c

Quadratic functions are characterized by a linear rate of change, so the rate of change of the rate of change (the second derivative) of a quadratic function is constant. Reasoning about the vertex form of a quadratic allows deducing that a quadratic has a maximum or minimum value and that if the zeros of the quadratic are real, they are symmetric about the x-coordinate of the maximum or minimum point.

When we put a "general" quadratic equation that is in standard form into vertex form and then use reasoning to find its roots, we derive the quadratic formula (Essential Understanding 3c). The process that we use is often called "completing the square."

Before we consider the general case of a quadratic function of the form $y = ax^2 + bx + c$, let's complete the square in the case of a quadratic function of the form $y = x^2 + bx + c$, where b and c are constants. This case is nicely illustrated with area pictures. Starting with $x^2 + bx + c$, which is illustrated in figure 1.18, we want to put the quadratic in the form $(x - h)^2 + k$, which has a square term that involves x and a constant term.

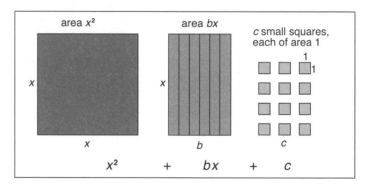

Fig. 1.18. Illustrating the quadratic $x^2 + bx + c$

Pictorially, we can make our quadratic more like a square if we split the bx term in half and move a portion of the c term to complete a square as shown in figure 1.19. We can see both pictorially and algebraically that

$$x^2 + bx + c = \left(x + \frac{b}{2}\right)^2 + \left(c - \frac{b^2}{4}\right).$$

Turning to the general case of $ax^2 + bx + c$, we can say that since

$$a\left(x + \frac{b}{2a}\right)^2 = ax^2 + bx + \frac{b^2}{4a},$$

it follows that

$$ax^2 + bx + c = a\left(x + \frac{b}{2a}\right)^2 + \left(c - \frac{b^2}{4a}\right).$$

By applying our previous reasoning on roots of quadratics in vertex form, we deduce that the roots of our quadratic are given by the familiar quadratic formula:

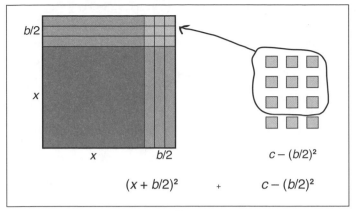

Fig. 1.19. Moving portions of $x^2 + bx + c$ to complete a square

$$x = -\frac{b}{2a} \pm \frac{\sqrt{b^2 - 4ac}}{2a} \quad \text{or} \quad x = \frac{-b \pm \sqrt{b^2 - 4ac}}{2a}.$$

This result demonstrates Essential Understanding 3c.

Exponential functions

Exponential functions describe many real-world situations that involve growth or decay, including the following:

- The accumulation of compound interest (amount as a function of time)

- Unrestricted population growth (population as a function of time)

- The decay of radioactive elements (amount as a function of time)

- Depreciation in the value of an object, such as a car (value as a function of time)

As in quadratic functions, in exponential functions the rate of change is not constant but changes. Exponential functions are characterized by a rate of change that is proportional to the value of the function (Essential Understanding 3d). It is this aspect of the rate of change of exponential functions that plays a major role in determining the kinds of real-world situations that exponential functions model, thus illustrating Essential Understanding 3a.

Contexts in which the rate of change is proportional to the function

Suppose that a population—of people, animals, or even bacteria in a Petri dish—has plenty of food, water, space, and other necessary

Essential Understanding 3d

Exponential functions are characterized by a rate of change that is proportional to the value of the function. It is a property of exponential functions that whenever the input is increased by 1 unit, the output is multiplied by a constant factor. Exponential functions connect multiplication to addition through the equation $a^{b+c} = (a^b)(a^c)$.

Essential Understanding 3a

Members of a family of functions share the same type of rate of change. This characteristic rate of change determines the kinds of real-world phenomena that the functions in the family can model.

resources, as well as no major predators. Over a given span of time, we would expect a large population to add more members to it than a smaller population. Because each couple is likely to produce a certain number of offspring, more couples ought to yield more new members for the population than fewer couples would. For example, if a population has 40,000 people and adds 2,000 people over the span of a year, then, if all conditions remain the same, we would expect the population to add *more than* 2,000 new people the following year, because 42,000 people should generate more growth than 40,000 people.

But we can describe the growth of an unrestricted population even more precisely. For each species, the portion of the species that is able to reproduce should produce offspring at a characteristic average rate, depending on factors such as fertility and gestational period for the species. Again, we are assuming that the population has plenty of food, water, space, and other necessary resources, and no predators. So in a stable, long-term situation where unrestricted growth is possible, the rate at which the population grows ought to be a fixed percentage of the population itself. For example, a population might increase by 5 percent each year, which means that the rate of change of the population is proportional to the population.

Consider again the situation in part (*b*) of Reflect 1.12, in which the town of Smallville (pop. 40,000) will experience a growth rate of 5 percent per year over the next 20 years. This means that each year, the next year's population will be 5 percent more than the current year's population. In other words, we have a recursive rule for the population, $P(T)$, after T years—namely, $P(T + 1) = P(T) + 0.05 \cdot P(T)$, or, by combining the terms on the right, $P(T + 1) = 1.05 \cdot P(T)$, which is a rule that describes a geometric sequence. We can create a table of (approximate) values to represent this situation, which shows that for each year that passes, the population P is multiplied by a constant amount (1.05). Figure 1.20 shows such a table.

We can also use the recursive rule $P(T + 1) = P(T) + 0.05 \cdot P(T)$ to see that the rate of change of the population is proportional to the population. Because $P(T)$ and $P(T + 1)$ refer to populations 1 year apart, the difference $P(T + 1) - P(T)$ is also the (average) rate of change of the population (from year T to year $T + 1$). So, since $P(T + 1) - P(T) = 0.05 \cdot P(T)$, the rate of change of the population is 0.05 times the population, regardless of what the population is at the time. In other words, the rate of change of the population is proportional to the population, with constant of proportionality 0.05 (Essential Understanding 3*d*).

Because each entry in the right-hand column of the table in figure 1.20 is 1.05 times the previous entry, the table exhibits a geometric sequence. On the basis of our earlier study of geometric

➡ Essential Understanding 3*d*

Exponential functions are characterized by a rate of change that is proportional to the value of the function. It is a property of exponential functions that whenever the input is increased by 1 unit, the output is multiplied by a constant factor. Exponential functions connect multiplication to addition through the equation $a^{b+c} = (a^b)(a^c)$.

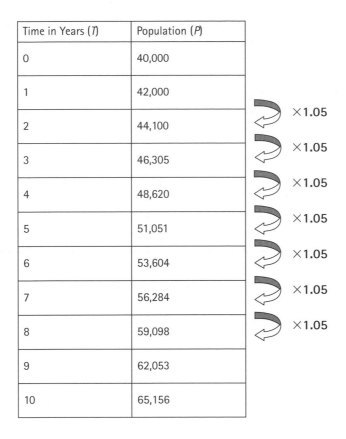

Time in Years (*T*)	Population (*P*)
0	40,000
1	42,000
2	44,100
3	46,305
4	48,620
5	51,051
6	53,604
7	56,284
8	59,098
9	62,053
10	65,156

Fig. 1.20. A table of values showing that for each year, the population *P* is multiplied by a constant, 1.05

sequences, we can see that a formula for the predicted population, *P*, of Smallville, in terms of *T*, the number of years from now, is $P(T) = 40{,}000(1.05)^T$. Note that the nature of the rate of change of the function determined the type of formula that the function has (Essential Understanding 2*a*).

Defining and characterizing exponential functions

In the preceding section, we derived the formula for the population of Smallville: $P(T) = 40{,}000(1.05)^T$. In our analysis, the input values for *T* were positive integers, but the formula for *P*(*T*) makes sense even when we put in values for *T* that are not integers. The function $P(T) = 40{,}000(1.05)^T$, where *T* is allowed to run over all real numbers, is an example of an exponential function. In general, we define the exponential functions to be the functions that can be represented in this way: $f(x) = a \cdot b^x$, where *b* > 0. We showed previously that every geometric sequence has a formula of the form $A \cdot b^N$ for the *N*th term, where *A* and *b* are constant. Therefore, every geometric sequence is an exponential function for which the domain is restricted to the positive integers (Essential Understanding 3*g*).

Essential
Understanding 2a

For functions that map real numbers to real numbers, certain patterns of covariation, or patterns in how two variables change together, indicate membership in a particular family of functions and determine the type of formula that the function has.

Essential
Understanding 3g

Geometric sequences can be thought of as exponential functions whose domains are the positive integers.

→ Essential
Understanding 3d

*Exponential
functions are
characterized by a
rate of change that is
proportional to the
value of the function.
It is a property
of exponential
functions that
whenever the input
is increased by 1
unit, the output is
multiplied by a
constant factor.
Exponential
functions connect
multiplication to
addition through
the equation*
$a^{b+c} = (a^b)(a^c)$.

Previously, we saw that the (average) rate of change of the population of Smallville over any 1-year interval is proportional to the population. Similarly, for any exponential function, the (average) rate of change of the function over any 1-unit interval is proportional to the function. By using calculus, we could show that every exponential function also has an *instantaneous* rate of change that is proportional to the function. In other words, we could use calculus to show that if $f(x)$ is an exponential function, then there is a constant of proportionality, k, such that $f'(x) = k \cdot f(x)$ (where $f'(x)$ is the derivative). We could also use calculus to show that if $f(x)$ is a function whose rate of change is proportional to the function, then $f(x)$ is an exponential function. Thus, exponential functions are characterized by an instantaneous rate of change that is proportional to the function (Essential Understanding 3d). Situations in which amounts increase or decrease at a rate proportional to the amount present are modeled by exponential functions, illustrating Essential Understanding 3a.

Graphs of exponential functions

For an exponential function, $f(x) = a \cdot b^x$, the parameter a is the function's y-intercept, and the parameter b is called the *base* of the function. The base, b, determines the rate of increase or decrease of the function. Reflect 1.26 explores the impact of different positive bases on exponential functions.

Reflect 1.26

Consider exponential functions represented by $f(x) = a \cdot b^x$, where $b > 0$.

For what values of b will the function *decrease* as x increases?

For what values of b will the function *increase* as x increases?

→ Essential
Understanding 3a

*Members of a family
of functions share
the same type of
rate of change. This
characteristic rate of
change determines
the kinds of real-
world phenomena
that the functions in
the family can model.*

Exponential functions decrease as x increases if the base, b, is between 0 and 1. Moreover, the smaller b is, the faster the rate of decrease will be. Consider the graphs in figure 1.21, corresponding to $y = (1/2)^x$ and $y = (1/10)^x$. Note that the function with the larger base, $y = (1/2)^x$, decreases more slowly than $y = (1/10)^x$, thus illustrating that the links between algebraic and graphical representations of a function have special importance to us when we are studying change (Essential Understanding 5d).

When the base, b, of an exponential function is 1, the function is a constant function whose output is a for every input. When $b > 1$, the function grows as x increases. This case was illustrated above in the population example. Larger bases give rise to faster growth rates. In the population example, the base was 1.05, and

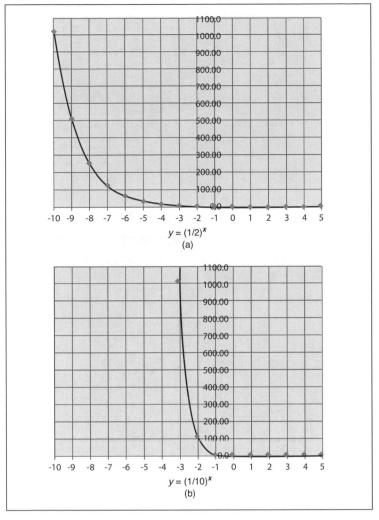

Essential
Understanding 5d

Links between algebraic and graphical representations of functions are especially important in studying relationships and change.

Fig. 1.21. Graphs illustrating growth for (*a*) $y = (1/2)^x$ and (*b*) $y = (1/10^x)$

after 20 years, the population of Smallville would be 106,132. If the population of Smallville increased by 10 percent each year, after 20 years it would be 269,100. Graphs depicting these two rates of population growth appear in figure 1.22.

Although the graph corresponding to $P = 40,000 \cdot (1.05)^T$ might appear to be somewhat linear, it is increasing exponentially—albeit at a much slower rate than $P = 40,000 \cdot (1.10)^T$ is increasing. In both cases, output values for P exhibit a multiplicative growth pattern with respect to unit changes in T. We can zoom in on a small piece of the graph corresponding to $P = 40,000 \cdot (1.05)^T$ to see the growth pattern, as in figure 1.23. As time goes on (as T increases), this graph will climb faster and faster. Although this function appears to be climbing slowly at first, eventually it will climb very quickly.

➡️ Essential
Understanding 3*d*

*Exponential functions
are characterized by
a rate of change that
is proportional to the
value of the function.
It is a property of
exponential func-
tions that whenever
the input is increased
by 1 unit, the output
is multiplied by a
constant factor. Expo-
nential functions con-
nect multiplication to
addition through
the equation
$a^{b+c} = (a^b)(a^c)$.*

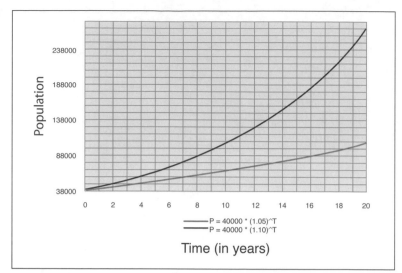

Fig. 1.22. Graphs showing growth rates of 5 percent (colored) and 10 percent (black) in a population

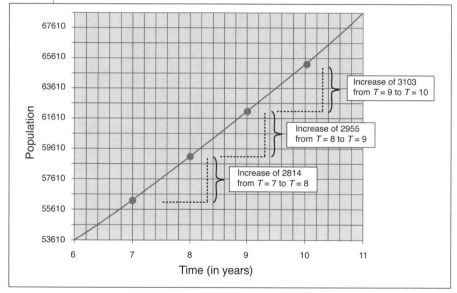

Fig. 1.23. Zooming in on a portion of the colored graph showing a 5 percent growth rate in figure 1.22

Graphs of exponential functions and the identity $b^{(u+v)} = b^u \cdot b^v$

The important identity $b^{(u+v)} = b^u \cdot b^v$, which is true for all real numbers u and v and all positive b, shows that exponential functions
connect addition to multiplication (Essential Understanding
3*d*). This identity also connects the arithmetic mean ($\frac{m+n}{2}$) to the
geometric mean ($\sqrt{m \cdot n}$), as you will see in Reflect 1.27.

Reflect 1.27

Given an exponential function $f(x) = a \cdot b^x$ for which $a > 0$ and $b > 0$, and given real numbers r, s, and t such that s is halfway between r and t (i.e., s is the arithmetic mean of r and t, namely, $s = \dfrac{r+t}{2}$), show that $f(s)$ is the geometric mean of $f(r)$ and $f(t)$. That is, show that $f(s) = \sqrt{f(r) \cdot f(t)}$.

The interesting fact that the geometric mean is less than the arithmetic mean is visible in graphs of exponential functions. When you look at the graphs of those exponential functions $f(x) = a \cdot b^x$ for which $a > 0$ and $b > 0$, you may notice that all of them curve upward. In fact, for any two points on such an exponential function, the portion of the graph that lies between the points is *below* the line connecting the points, as shown in the example in figure 1.24. In particular, for x-coordinates $x = r$, $x = s$, $x = t$ such that s is halfway between r and t, $f(s)$ is less than halfway between $f(r)$ and $f(t)$.

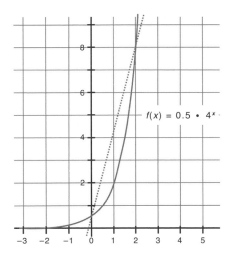

Fig. 1.24. The geometric mean is clearly less than the arithmetic mean.

Trigonometric functions

The trigonometric functions are important for two reasons: (1) they provide a way to find unknown lengths in terms of known lengths and known angles and thus are useful in a variety of applications (Essential Understanding 3e), and (2) they are the most natural periodic functions, and they can be used to approximate any periodic function. This section will focus on a few unusual examples that illustrate point (1) about trigonometric functions.

Essential Understanding 3e

Trigonometric functions are natural and fundamental examples of periodic functions. For angles between 0 and 90 degrees, the trigonometric functions can be defined as the ratios of side lengths in right triangles; these functions are well defined because the ratios of side lengths are equivalent in similar triangles. For general angles, the sine and cosine functions can be viewed as the y- and x-coordinates of points on circles or as the projection of circular motion onto the y- and x-axes.

Defining the trigonometric functions

In their most basic form, the core trigonometric functions, sine and cosine, and the related tangent function (as well as the secondary trigonometric functions cosecant, secant, and cotangent) are all defined in terms of right triangles. Given a right triangle that has an angle θ, we have the familiar definitions:

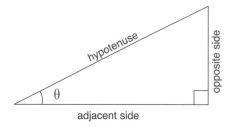

$$\sin(\theta) = \frac{opposite}{hypotenuse}, \quad \cos(\theta) = \frac{adjacent}{hypotenuse}, \quad \tan(\theta) = \frac{opposite}{adjacent}$$

In each case, *hypotenuse* stands for the length of the hypotenuse of the right triangle, and *adjacent* and *opposite* stand for the lengths of the sides of the right triangle that are adjacent to and opposite from the angle θ, respectively.

A natural question arises when we define the trigonometric functions in this way: do these functions depend only on the angle θ, as the notation indicates, or do they depend on the particular triangle that we chose with θ as one of its angles? After all, given an acute angle θ, we could have chosen many right triangles with θ as one of their angles—some large, some small, as in figure 1.25. The key to answering this question lies in triangle similarity, as Reflect 1.28 asks you to investigate.

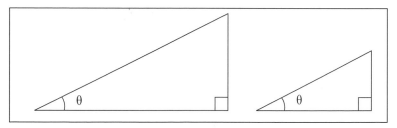

Fig. 1.25. Two right triangles that have the same acute angle θ but different side lengths

Reflect 1.28

Why is triangle similarity crucial for defining the trigonometric functions?

According to the angle-angle-angle criterion for triangle similarity, any two right triangles that have the same acute angle θ must be similar. The angle-angle-angle criterion applies because each triangle has an angle θ, a 90-degree angle, and an angle of (90 − θ) degrees, since the sum of the angles in a triangle is 180 degrees. Because ratios between corresponding sides are equivalent in similar triangles, the value of a trigonometric function depends only on the angle and not on the particular triangle that we chose.

If we used only the definitions above, we would limit the domain of each of the trigonometric functions to the open interval (0, 90), assuming that we were measuring angles in degrees. The familiar way to extend the domain of the trigonometric functions is to define these functions in terms of the *x*- and *y*-coordinates of a point on a circle of radius 1, centered at the origin. Given an angle θ, consider the ray from the origin that makes angle θ with the positive *x*-axis. This ray intersects the circle at a point, as figure 1.26 illustrates.

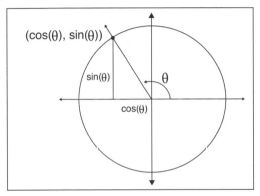

Fig. 1.26. Cosine and sine as coordinates of a point on the unit circle

Sin(θ) is defined to be the *y*-coordinate of this point, cos(θ) is defined to be its *x*-coordinate, and the other trigonometric functions are defined in terms of sin(θ) and cos(θ), as appropriate. In other words, sin(θ) and cos(θ) are defined so that the point that has polar coordinates (1, θ) has rectangular coordinates (cos(θ), sin(θ)). Viewed in this way, the sine and cosine are essentially projections onto the *y*- and *x*-axes of points on a circle of radius 1 centered at the origin (Essential Understanding 3e). If we scale such a circle so that it has radius *r*, then the *x*- and *y*-coordinates of a point on the circle that has polar coordinates (*r*, θ) are *r*cos(θ) and *r*sin(θ).

Degrees versus radians

Note that since we can describe angles in terms of degrees or in terms of radians, we must make clear which unit we are using when we work with the trigonometric functions. When we use radians, we describe the size of an angle in terms of the length of a portion of a

---

Essential ⬅
Understanding 3e

Trigonometric functions are natural and fundamental examples of periodic functions. For angles between 0 and 90 degrees, the trigonometric functions can be defined as the ratios of side lengths in right triangles; these functions are well defined because the ratios of side lengths are equivalent in similar triangles. For general angles, the sine and cosine functions can be viewed as the y- and x-coordinates of points on circles or as the projection of circular motion onto the y- and x-axes.

unit circle, thus linking angle measure to length. That is, if a circle of radius 1 is centered at the vertex of a given angle, then the angle cuts off an arc on the circle, and the length of this arc is the measure of the angle in radians.

Because radian measure is tied to the lengths of arcs on circles, it is a more natural measure of angle size than degrees. In degrees, a straight angle is assigned the rather arbitrary value of 180 degrees, which is, however, convenient for many calculations because of its many small factors.

An application of sine and cosine: Circular arches

The sine and cosine arise naturally when we consider arcs of circles. What are some real-world contexts in which arcs on circles come into play? One is architecture, which frequently uses circular arches. To describe a circular arch, architects can use the width and height of the arch, attributes that are identified in figure 1.27. A circular arch

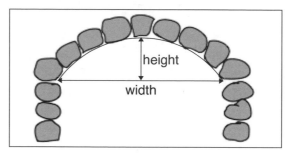

Fig. 1.27. The width and height of a circular arch

is based on an arc on a circle, so the width and height of the arch depend on the arc's angle and the circle's radius. Reflect 1.29 invites consideration of the relationship among these elements.

Reflect 1.29

Describe the width and height of a circular arch as a function of the radius and arc angle of the arc on which the arch is based.

Suppose that we are given an arc on a circle of radius r. We can place the arc on the circle so that the positive x-axis divides the arc in half, as in figure 1.28. If the angle of the original arc is θ, then the angle of each half-arc is $\frac{\theta}{2}$, and the x- and y-coordinates of the upper endpoint on the arc are $r\cos\left(\frac{\theta}{2}\right)$ and $r\sin\left(\frac{\theta}{2}\right)$, respectively.

Thus, given an arch that is an arc of angle θ on a circle of radius r, we can determine that the width of the arch is

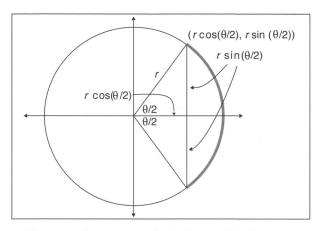

Fig. 1.28. An arc on a circle, bisected by the *x*-axis

$2r\sin\left(\dfrac{\theta}{2}\right)$ and the height of the arch is $r - r\cos\left(\dfrac{\theta}{2}\right)$. By viewing arches in terms of lengths and angles in a circle, we can use trigonometric functions to describe the width and height of an arch, thus illustrating Essential Understanding 3*e*.

An application of sine and cosine: Crocheting a hemispherical cap

To crochet a cap in the shape of a hemisphere, like the one shown in figure 1.29, you can start at the top of the hat and crochet concentric circular rows. Each crocheted circular row consists of a number of stitches—a number that grows as the rows progress, so that each circular row of the cap is a little larger than the previous row.

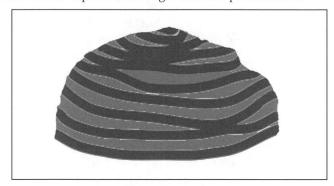

Fig. 1.29. A side view of a crocheted hemispherical cap made of concentric circular rows

For people who crochet hemispherical caps, a natural question is, How many stitches are needed in each row? Of course, the number of stitches needed in each row depends on the size of the cap and the thickness of the yarn. Suppose you want to crochet a hemispherical cap with a circumference of 24 inches, and you have

Essential
Understanding 3e

Trigonometric functions are natural and fundamental examples of periodic functions. For angles between 0 and 90 degrees, the trigonometric functions can be defined as the ratios of side lengths in right triangles; these functions are well defined because the ratios of side lengths are equivalent in similar triangles. For general angles, the sine and cosine functions can be viewed as the y- and x-coordinates of points on circles or as the projection of circular motion onto the y- and x-axes.

chosen yarn so that each stitch is 2/5 inch wide and 2/5 inch high. Reflect 1.30 restates the natural question—How many stitches are needed in each row?—in a different way.

Reflect 1.30

What is a function that describes approximately how many stitches you will need to crochet in row N of the hemispherical cap?

Because the cap is half of a sphere of circumference 24 inches, and the arc from the top of the cap to the edge is a quarter-circle, the length of the cap from the top to the edge must be $24 \div 4$, or 6, inches. So, you will need to crochet $6 \div \frac{2}{5}$, or 15, rows to make the cap. Because each row is a circle, the length of the row is the circumference of that circle, which is $2\pi \cdot r(N)$, where $r(N)$ is the radius of the circle that is row N. Because each stitch is 2/5 inch wide, the number of stitches that you will need in row N is $\frac{5}{2} \cdot 2\pi \cdot r(N) = 5\pi \cdot r(N)$. Reflect 1.31 explores $r(N)$.

Reflect 1.31

What is a formula for $r(N)$, the radius of the Nth row of the hemispherical cap?

On the basis of that formula, what is a formula for the number of stitches needed in the Nth row of the cap?

It is interesting to note that Reflect 1.30 and Reflect 1.31 about a crocheted cap are closely related to Reflect 1.29 about the width of an arch. Imagine cutting the cap in half, straight down through the top. The cut edge forms a semicircle, and the portion from the top of the cap to a bottom edge forms a quarter-circle. This quarter-circle is formed from 15 rows, so each row takes up 6° of arc. Imagine placing the cut semicircle in the plane so that the top of the cap is on the positive x-axis and the finished bottom edges are on the y-axis. Each row that is crocheted creates a larger and larger arc, half of which is above the x-axis and half below, as in figure 1.30.

After crocheting the Nth row, you have created a partial cap that makes an arc of $6N°$ on the portion above the x-axis (since each row contributes 6 degrees of arc). Because the circumference of the full circle is 24 inches, its radius is $\frac{12}{\pi}$ inches. So, as indicated in figure 1.30, the radius of the Nth row is $\frac{12}{\pi} \sin(6N)$ inches. The number of 2/5-inch stitches in the Nth row should therefore be approximately $5\pi \cdot \frac{12}{\pi} \cdot \sin(6N)$, or $60\sin(6N)$.

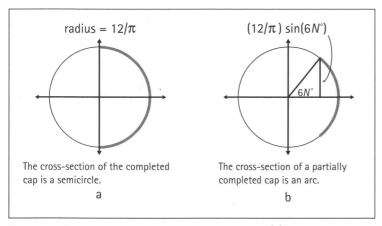

The cross-section of the completed cap is a semicircle.

a

The cross-section of a partially completed cap is an arc.

b

Fig. 1.30. Cross sections of a hemispherical cap, (*a*) completed and (*b*) in progress

So, by using angles and lengths in a circle, we are able to describe the number of stitches needed to crochet a cap in terms of trigonometric functions, once again illustrating Essential Understanding 3*e*. Although people who crochet caps may not feel the need to use trigonometry to help them, it is still interesting and surprising that crocheting can be described by trigonometry!

An application of sine and cosine: Making a pattern for an oblique cylinder

It is easy to make a right cylinder without bases: just attach a pair of opposite sides of a rectangular piece of paper. But how can you make an oblique cylinder from a piece of paper? One way to make an oblique cylinder is to start with a right cylinder and cut off portions of the top and bottom, as if slicing the cylinder with a pair of parallel planes that are neither parallel nor perpendicular to the bases of the right cylinder, as pictured in figure 1.31.

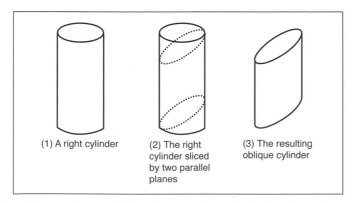

(1) A right cylinder

(2) The right cylinder sliced by two parallel planes

(3) The resulting oblique cylinder

Fig. 1.31. Slicing a right cylinder with parallel planes to make an oblique cylinder

Essential Understanding 3e

Trigonometric functions are natural and fundamental examples of periodic functions. For angles between 0 and 90 degrees, the trigonometric functions can be defined as the ratios of side lengths in right triangles; these functions are well defined because the ratios of side lengths are equivalent in similar triangles. For general angles, the sine and cosine functions can be viewed as the y- and x-coordinates of points on circles or as the projection of circular motion onto the y- and x-axes.

So, to make an oblique cylinder out of paper, you could first take a rectangular piece of paper and tape a pair of opposite sides together to make a right circular cylinder. Now imagine slicing the paper cylinder with a pair of parallel planes to form an oblique cylinder, as in figure 1.32. Finally, imagine removing the tape and unrolling the oblique paper cylinder so that you have a flat piece of paper again, but now with cut edges at the top and bottom of the paper. Reflect 1.32 invites you to consider the cut edges.

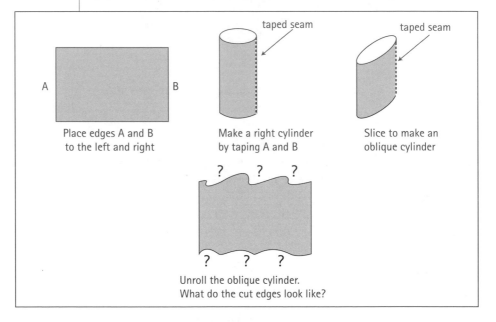

Fig. 1.32. Unrolling an oblique cylinder made by slicing a right cylinder

Reflect 1.32

What do you think the cut edges of the piece of paper would look like?

Could you describe these cut edges with the aid of a function? If so, how? What characteristics should such a function have?

Before continuing to investigate the questions in Reflect 1.32 theoretically, you might like to investigate them empirically. If you happen to have a wooden dowel and saw available, wrap a rectangular piece of paper around the dowel so that the paper forms a right cylinder. You can wrap the paper around the rod several times, forming (approximately) several concentric paper cylinders. Use the saw to make an oblique (but straight) cut through the dowel rod and the paper. The cut should lie in a plane that is neither parallel nor perpendicular to the ends of the dowel. (If you do not have access to a dowel and saw, roll up a piece of paper and cut it with scissors to simulate a saw's cut. Note, however, that you cannot do this by flattening the paper roll first and then cutting.) Unroll the paper and observe the cut edge. Reflect 1.33 encourages you to reconsider your thinking in Reflect 1.32 in light of your experimentation.

Reflect 1.33

What does the cut edge look like? Does it look like the graph of a familiar function?

Describe the cut edge as the graph of a function and explain theoretically why your function must describe the cut edge.

If you unroll an oblique paper cylinder created by slicing a right circular cylinder with a pair of parallel planes, then the cut edges will resemble a sine or cosine curve. The sine or cosine curve will be especially apparent if you wrapped several layers of paper around a dowel, as described above.

Why should the cut edge be a sine or cosine curve? The cut edge must be the graph of a periodic function because locations on the paper that lie over the same point on the dowel rod are the same height above the original edge of the paper. But this does not prove that the cut edge is a sine or cosine function. Furthermore, how do we even model the cut edge of a paper roll with a specific function? This example provides a good opportunity to take a real-world situation, make specific quantitative assumptions about it (as in the situation of crocheting a cap), and then model the situation mathematically with a function. Reflect 1.34 explores this process.

Reflect 1.34

Make specific quantitative assumptions about the paper roll that forms a right cylinder, and make specific assumptions about one of the oblique planes that cuts the paper roll, making a base of an oblique cylinder.

Use these assumptions to describe the height of the cut edge above the original edge of the paper at a base of the cylinder.

In the discussion that follows, we'll make some assumptions that might be different from yours, so that our function describing the cut edge may be somewhat different from yours. First, we'll take the radius of the right cylinder to be 1 unit, and we'll view the cylinder as standing on the xy-plane so that its bottom base is a circle of radius 1 centered at the origin, as in figure 1.33.

Let's view the rectangular piece of paper as wrapped counterclockwise to form the cylinder so that the bottom left corner of the paper is at the point $(1, 0, 0)$. When the rectangular piece of paper

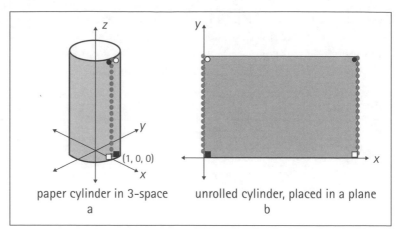

Fig. 1.33. A paper cylinder (a) in 3-space and (b) placed in a plane after unrolling

is unrolled, let's view it as placed in the first quadrant of another coordinate plane so that the lower left corner of the paper is at the origin and the bottom edge of the paper, which wraps around the base of the right cylinder, lies along the positive x-axis, as shown in figure 1.33. Now, let's assume that the plane slicing the cylinder to make an oblique base has equation $z = x + 1$ (if we made it just $z = x$, without adding 1, the plane would miss much of the paper). Reflect 1.35 probes the usefulness of these assumptions.

Reflect 1.35

Using our assumptions, consider the cut edge of the paper, unrolled and placed in the xy-plane as described, as the graph of a function.

Give a formula for this function and explain why the function has this formula.

To describe the cut edge of the paper as the graph of a function, we must find the height of the cut edge above the original bottom edge, and we must translate between the cylinder in 3-space (standing on the xy-plane) and the unrolled paper in the first quadrant of another xy-plane. This translation will be very natural if we work with cylindrical coordinates in the cylinder's 3-space—in other words, if we use polar coordinates instead of x and y, while using the z-coordinate as usual. The plane that slices the cylinder is given in rectangular coordinates by $z = x + 1$, which becomes $z = r\cos(\theta) + 1$ in cylindrical coordinates. Because $r = 1$ for the cylinder, the height, z, of the cut edge is given by $z = \cos(\theta) + 1$. Now, let's translate into the xy-plane of the unrolled paper. Assuming that we are using radians to measure angles for the cylindrical coordinates of the cylinder's 3-space, these angles become "x" in the xy-plane. (Choosing the radius of the cylinder to be 1 made this especially easy; if we had chosen a different radius, we would have to multiply x by it here.) Therefore, when the paper is unrolled in the plane, the height, y, of its cut edge is given by $y = \cos(x) + 1$. So, if you want to make a paper pattern for an oblique cylinder, you can draw two cosine curves on a piece of paper, with one curve shifted up from the other. To form the oblique cylinder, you can simply cut along those curves, and then join the other two uncut edges of the paper.

If you sew, you have probably encountered a pattern for an oblique cylinder. A garment's sleeve is generally shaped like one—especially the portion at the shoulder.

Trigonometric functions have many interesting and important aspects that we have not discussed, including the identities concerning sines and cosines of sums of angles. For a brief summary of key ideas in trigonometry, see Hill (2007).

Combining and Transforming Functions

Big Idea 4. *Functions can be combined by adding, subtracting, multiplying, dividing, and composing them. Functions sometimes have inverses. Functions can often be analyzed by viewing them as made from other functions.*

An important technique that is used throughout mathematics is to analyze a mathematical object or situation by taking it apart, analyzing the pieces, and putting the pieces back together to draw a conclusion. For example, the distributive property allows us to break a multi-digit multiplication problem into several one-digit multiplication problems, and the volume of an object can often be determined by breaking the object (mentally) into pieces and applying volume formulas to the pieces. Functions can be combined, broken apart, and transformed in several different ways, allowing us to analyze functions and to see relationships among graphs of functions. In calculus, it is useful to be able to decompose functions because there are rules for finding derivatives of sums, differences, products, quotients, and compositions of functions.

Adding, subtracting, multiplying, and dividing functions

A function can be a sum or difference of other functions, such as $\sin(x) - \cos(x)$, or it can be a product or quotient of other functions, such as $\frac{x}{e^x}$. A function can even be a combination of sums, differences, products, and quotients, such as $\frac{x-1}{x+1} - x\sin(x)$.

As expressed in Essential Understanding 4a, given two functions f and g that map to the real numbers and have the same domain, we can form new functions, $f + g$, $f - g$, $f \cdot g$, and $\frac{f}{g}$, defined by the following rules:

$$(f + g)(x) = f(x) + g(x) \qquad (f - g)(x) = f(x) - g(x)$$

$$(f \cdot g)(x) = f(x) \cdot g(x) \qquad \left(\frac{f}{g}\right)(x) = \frac{f(x)}{g(x)}$$

→ Essential Understanding 4a

Functions that have the same domain and that map to the real numbers can be added, subtracted, multiplied, or divided (which may change the domain).

These functions all have the same domain as f and g, except that those x for which $g(x) = 0$ may need to be removed for the domain of $\frac{f}{g}$.

Adding and multiplying by a constant function are of special interest because their effects on the graph of a function are easy to describe. Reflect 1.36 explores these effects.

Reflect 1.36

What is the effect on the graph of a function of adding a constant function?

What is the effect on the graph of a function of multiplying by a constant function? For example, what is the effect on the graph of $f(x) = x^2$ of multiplying by the constant function $g(x) = 2$, or $g(x) = 0.5$, or $g(x) = -2$?

If we add a constant function, $g(x) = c$ (where c is a constant), to a function f whose domain lies in the real numbers, then the graph of the resulting sum function, $f + g$, is simply shifted vertically by $|c|$ units—up if c is positive and down if c is negative. So, for example, as c runs over all real numbers, the graphs of $y = x^2 + c$ run over all vertical shifts of the graph of $y = x^2$.

Multiplying a function by a constant function scales the graph of the function vertically, but not horizontally, and also reflects the graph over the x-axis if the constant is negative. As we see in figure 1.34, the graphs of $y = c \cdot x^2$ (i.e., $(f \cdot g)(x)$, where $f(x) = c$ and $g(x) = x^2$) are all different for different constant values of c.

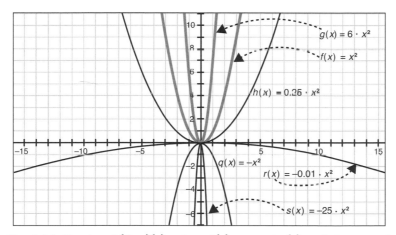

Fig. 1.34. Graphs of $(f \cdot g)(x)$, where $f(x) = c$ and $g(x) = x^2$, for several different values of c

It is interesting to note that for positive values of c, these graphs can be obtained by "zooming in" or "zooming out" on the graph of $y = x^2$, or by rescaling the x- and y-axes. To see why, let k be a positive constant and let D_k be the dilation by k that is centered at the origin and maps the plane to the plane by $D_k(x, y) = (kx, ky)$. You will notice that D_k takes the square "window" in the plane that is given by $(-1 \le x \le 1, -1 \le y \le 1)$ to the "window" given by $(-k \le x \le k, -k \le y \le k)$, so for $k > 1$, D_k has the effect of "zooming out," and for $k < 1$, D_k has the effect of "zooming in." Reflect 1.37 invites you to explore these results.

Reflect 1.37

Use a graphing calculator to help you determine the effect of D_2 (dilation by a factor of 2, centered at the origin) on several points on the graph of $y = x^2$. Which graph of the form $y = c \cdot x^2$ do the image points lie on?

Determine the effect of $D_{\frac{1}{2}}$ (dilation by a factor of $\frac{1}{2}$, centered at the origin) on several points on the graph of $y = x^2$. Which graph of the form $y = c \cdot x^2$ do the image points lie on?

Notice that D_k takes points on the graph of $y = x^2$, which are points of the form (x, x^2), to the points $(kx, kx^2) = (kx, \frac{1}{k}(kx)^2)$, which are the points on the graph of $y = \frac{1}{k}x^2$. So, every graph of the form $y = c \cdot x^2$, where c is a positive constant, can be viewed as a scaled version of the graph of $y = x^2$. Therefore, if we graph $y = x^2$ but then remove the scales on the axes, we can no longer tell which graph of the form $y = x^2$ the graph represents.

Figure 1.35 shows graphs of $y = x^2$ and $y = \left(\frac{1}{2}\right)x^2$. The two graphs $y = x^2$ and $y = \left(\frac{1}{2}\right)x^2$ look alike until we notice the scales on the axes.

Similarly, we can choose window settings (Xmin, Xmax, Ymin, and Ymax) on a graphing calculator so that the graph of $y = 4x^2$ looks like the graph of $y = x^2$. Figure 1.36 shows the results.

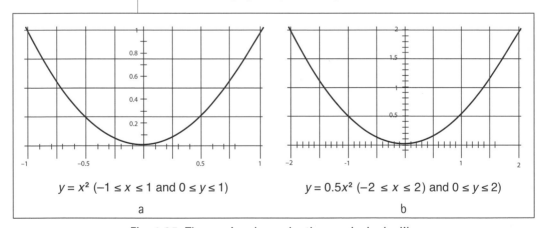

$y = x^2 \ (-1 \le x \le 1 \text{ and } 0 \le y \le 1)$ $y = 0.5x^2 \ (-2 \le x \le 2) \text{ and } 0 \le y \le 2)$

a   b

Fig. 1.35. The axes' scales make the graphs look alike.

Composition of functions

For two functions f and g, the *composition* of f and g, denoted as $f \circ g$, is the function that takes an input a to the output $f(g(a))$. We can think of the composition, $f \circ g$, of two functions f and g as first taking an input a to $g(a)$, and then taking $g(a)$ to $f(g(a))$. Symbolically, we can indicate the net effect of $f \circ g$ in the following way:

$$a \mapsto g(a) \mapsto f(g(a))$$

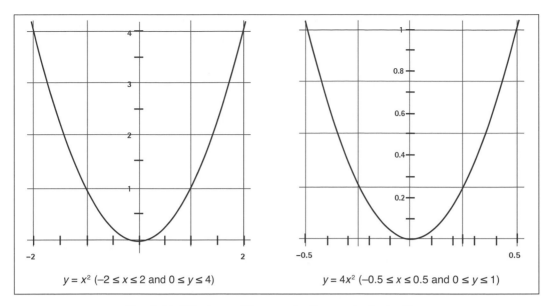

$y = x^2$ ($-2 \le x \le 2$ and $0 \le y \le 4$) $y = 4x^2$ ($-0.5 \le x \le 0.5$ and $0 \le y \le 1$)

Fig. 1.36. Window settings make the graphs look alike.

For example, if $f(x) = \sin(x)$ and $g(x) = 2x$, then $(f \circ g)(x) = f(g(x)) = \sin(g(x)) = \sin(2x)$. Reflect 1.38 poses a question about the composition of f and g.

Reflect 1.38

What requirements must be made of the functions f and g so that the definition of $f \circ g$ makes sense?

For $f \circ g$ to make sense, $g(a)$ must be in the domain of f for every element a in the domain of g (Essential Understanding 4b). In general, the *image* of g, which is the set of all $g(a)$ such that a is in the domain of g, must lie within the domain of f for us to be able to form the composition, $f \circ g$. In other words, for $f \circ g$ to be defined, we require

$$\text{image of } g \subseteq \text{domain of } f.$$

Essential Understanding 4b

Under appropriate conditions, functions can be composed.

Sometimes, to define $f \circ g$, we must restrict the domain of g. For example, if $f(x) = \dfrac{1}{x}$ and $g(x) = x - 2$, then we must restrict the domain of g to the set of all real numbers other than 2 for $(f \circ g)(x) = \dfrac{1}{x - 2}$ to be defined.

Calculus develops derivatives of basic functions such as the powers (x^n, where n is constant), $\sin(x)$, and e^x, as well as rules for determining derivatives of sums, differences, products, quotients, and compositions. Thus, by decomposing functions as sums, differences, products, quotients, and compositions, we can determine the derivatives of many functions.

Composing with "translating" and "scaling" functions to transform graphs

We have seen that when we add a constant function to a function, we shift the function's graph vertically, and that when we multiply a function by a constant function, we scale the function's graph vertically (and also reflect the graph over the x-axis if the constant is negative). We can also view adding a constant function to a function and multiplying a function by a constant function as the composition of functions.

For a real number k, let T_k and S_k be the functions mapping the real numbers to the real numbers, defined by $T_k(x) = x + k$ and $S_k(x) = kx$. Notice that to add the constant function k to a function f, we can form the function $T_k \circ f$, and to multiply the function f by the constant function k, we can form the function $S_k \circ f$. What happens if we compose these functions in the opposite order? This is the question that Reflect 1.39 investigates.

Reflect 1.39

a. If $f(x) = \sin(x)$, how is the graph of f related to the graphs of $f \circ T_{\pi/2}$ and $f \circ S_{1/3}$?

b. Think about the situation in part (*a*) more generally. Given a function f that maps the real numbers to the real numbers, how are the graphs of $f \circ T_k$ and $f \circ S_k$ related to the graph of f? Why are they related that way?

The graph of $f \circ T_k$ is the same as the graph of f except shifted horizontally: it is shifted to the left k units if k is positive, and shifted to the right $|k|$ units if k is negative. Because T_k adds k, these shifts may seem paradoxical, but since $(f \circ T_k)(a - k) = f(a - k + k) = f(a)$, the value of $f \circ T_k$ at $x = a - k$ is the same as the value of f at $x = a$.

Figure 1.37 shows the graphs of $f(x) = x^3$ and $g(x) = f(T_2(x)) = f(x + 2) = (x + 2)^3$. The graphs illustrate how the graph of f composed with T_2 shifts the graph of f to the left two units. For any a, $g(a) = f(a + 2)$. For example, $g(-2) = f(0) = 0$ and $g(0) = f(2) = 8$.

The graph of $f \circ S_k$ is obtained from the graph of f by scaling horizontally and also reflecting across the y-axis if k is negative. This horizontal scaling results because the value of $f \circ S_k$ at $x = a$ is the same as the value of f at $x = x \cdot a$. For example, figure 1.38 shows the graphs of $f(x) = x^3$ and $h(x) = f(S_2(x)) = f(2x) = 8x^3$. The graphs illustrate how the graph of f composed with S_2 "scales" the graph of f horizontally by a factor of 2. For any a, $h(a) = f(2a)$. For example, $h(0.5) = f(1) = 1$, and $h(1) = f(2) = 8$.

So, if we apply a translating or scaling function *after* a function f (i.e., forming $T_k \circ f$ or $S_k \circ f$), we translate or scale the graph

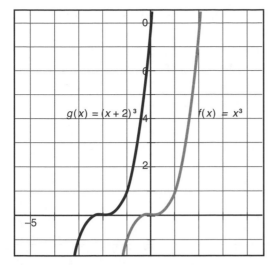

Fig. 1.37. Graphs of $f(x) = x^3$ and $g(x) = f(T_2(x)) = k(x + 2) = (x + 2)^3$

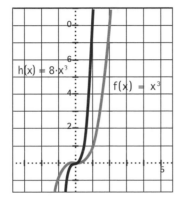

Fig. 1.38. Graphs of $f(x) = x^3$ and $h(x) = f(S_2(x)) = 8x^3$

of f vertically, but if we apply a translating or scaling function *be-fore* f (i.e., forming $f \circ T_k$ or $f \circ S_k$), we translate or scale the graph of f *horizontally*. The idea that composing a function with "shifting" and "scaling" functions changes the formula and graph of the function in predictable ways constitutes Essential Understanding 4c.

Inverses of functions

For a function f, the *inverse* of f, denoted f^{-1} (which looks deceptively like, but is not to be confused with, $\frac{1}{f}$), is the function such that $(f^{-1} \circ f)(a) = a$ for all a in the domain of f. Notice that f^{-1} "undoes" f because if f takes an element a to $f(a)$, then f^{-1} takes $f(a)$ back to a.

There is, however, a requirement of the function f for the definition of f^{-1} to make sense. If there are two distinct values a and b such that $f(a) = f(b)$, then $f^{-1}(f(a)) = f^{-1}(f(b))$ would need to be equal

Essential ← Understanding 4c

For functions that map the real numbers to the real numbers, composing a function with "shifting" or "scaling" functions changes the formula and graph of the function in readily predictable ways.

to both *a* and *b*, which is not possible if f^{-1} is to be a function. So, for a function *f* to have an inverse, there must not be any two distinct values *a* and *b*, such that $f(a) = f(b)$. In other words, *f* must be one-to-one to have an inverse (Essential Understanding 4d). Reflect 1.40 offers several functions for scrutiny.

Reflect 1.40

a. Determine whether functions *f*, *g*, *h*, and *zip* have inverses:

$$f(x) = x^2(x + 4) \qquad\qquad g(x) = x^{1/3}$$

x	−2	−1	0	1	2	3	4
h(*x*)	4	1	0	1	4	9	16

The function *zip* that maps any residential phone number to the zip code of its residence.

b. How could you use graphs of functions such as *f*, *g*, and *h* in part (*a*) to help you determine whether inverses exist?

 Essential Understanding 4d

Under appropriate conditions, functions have inverses. The logarithmic functions are the inverses of the exponential functions. The square root function is the inverse of the squaring function.

The function *g* is the only one-to-one function in Reflect 1.40. Why is this the case? One way to determine whether a function is one-to-one is to apply the "horizontal line test" to the graph of the function: If a horizontal line intersects a function's graph more than once, the function is not one-to-one. If a function is not one-to-one, then we can usually restrict the domain so that it becomes one-to-one and therefore has an inverse. For example, the squaring function shown in the table in Reflect 1.40 ($h(x) = x^2$) does not have an inverse because $h(a) = h(-a)$, but if we restrict the domain of the squaring function to the nonnegative real numbers, then the restricted function does have an inverse—namely, the square root function, $h^{-1}(x) = \sqrt{x}$. Explore the method suggested in Reflect 1.41 for determining whether or not a function has an inverse.

Reflect 1.41

To find the inverse of a function $y = f(x)$, a common method is to solve for *x* in terms of *y*.

Why does this method make sense?

Explain why the method makes sense in the case of $f(x) = x^3$, shown in the graph in figure 1.39.

If a function has a domain and range that lie within the real numbers and if the function has an inverse, then the graphs of the function and its inverse are reflections of each other across the

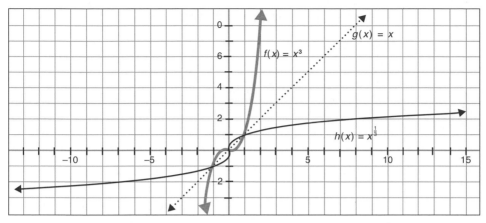

Fig. 1.39. Graphs of $f(x) = x^3$, $g(x) = x$, and $h(x) = x^{1/3}$

diagonal line $y = x$. Why? If we think of the original function as taking x to y, then the inverse takes y back to x. So, to find the inverse function, we should solve for x in terms of y. For example, if the original function is the squaring function (restricted to the non-negative real numbers), then it takes x to x^2, so $y = x^2$. The inverse function must take y back to x. Because $x = \sqrt{y}$, the inverse function takes y to $\sqrt{y}$. But if we want to express the inverse function in terms of the variable x instead of y, then we should replace x with y and y with x in the equation $y = x^2$ to obtain $x = y^2$, which we can solve for y as $y = \sqrt{x}$. The process of "replacing x with y and y with x" is really just the mapping $(x, y) \mapsto (y, x)$ from the plane to the plane that is a reflection across the diagonal line $y = x$.

One especially important family of inverse functions is the logarithms, which are the inverses of the exponential functions. Logarithms are defined only on positive real numbers, and they are defined by $\log_a(x) = y$ if $a^y = x$. In other words, $\log_a(x)$ is the exponent to which you must raise a to get x. So $\log_a(x)$ is the inverse of a^x. Logarithms have two key properties:

$$\log_a(b \cdot c) = \log_a(b) + \log_a(c) \quad \text{and} \quad \log_a(b^c) = c \cdot \log_a(b)$$

These properties follow from the related properties of exponential functions:

$$a^{b+c} = a^b \cdot a^c \quad \text{and} \quad a^{b \cdot c} = (a^b)^c$$

Historically, logarithms were an important computational tool because they convert multiplication to the easier operation of addition, and they convert exponentiation to the easier operation of multiplication. In the past, people used a table of logarithms to multiply large numbers quickly by looking up the logarithms of the factors, adding those values, and then looking up the value whose logarithm is the sum. It is interesting to note that logarithms were developed before exponentials (see Klein [1945]).

Multiple Representations of Functions

Big Idea 5. *Functions can be represented in multiple ways, including algebraic (symbolic), graphical, verbal, and tabular representations. Links among these different representations are important to studying relationships and change.*

➡ Essential Understanding 5*a*

Functions can be represented in various ways, including through algebraic means (e.g., equations), graphs, word descriptions, and tables.

As we have seen in previous sections, relationships may be represented in many different ways, including rules or formulas, tables, diagrams and graphs, and verbal descriptions. This important notion is captured in Essential Understanding 5*a*. Different representations of functions help us to gain insights into many aspects of relationships and change.

Some textbooks emphasize particular representations of functions more than others. For example, many algebra textbooks introduce functions to students as rules and graphs. In general, textbooks that present correspondence and ordered-pairs definitions tend to try to draw students' attention to graphical representations of functions. As Usiskin and colleagues explained,

> The ordered pair characterization of function is particularly appropriate for real functions because we can picture the ordered pairs in a *graph*. For this reason, some authors prefer to define a function as a correspondence and define the graph of a function to be the set of ordered pairs created by the correspondence. (Usiskin et al. 2003, p. 70)

Many introductory calculus textbooks portray functions primarily as formulas—the representation in which students learn to differentiate and integrate functions. Definition D in table 1.1 exemplifies this view of functions as formulas. The other calculus textbook definition in the table, definition H, uses the idea of input-output, which closely connects to a formulaic representation of function. The idea of input-output, sometimes depicted in the form of a "function machine," suggests that the input is affected somehow by the function to produce the output. Several other input-output definitions in table 1.1 appear in high school textbooks that relate the input-output analogy to function machines, tables, graphs, and rules. For example, the Interactive Mathematics Program curriculum (which gives definition C) introduces and emphasizes functions as in-out machines and in-out tables, for which students later generate corresponding rules and graphs.

Representing functions in multiple ways and analyzing functions from different perspectives are critical aspects of learning functions. NCTM's Standards recommend that high school students "understand relations and functions and select, convert flexibly among, and use various representations for them" (NCTM 2000, p. 294), including "tabular, symbolic, graphical, and verbal representations" (p. 296). To some extent, this focus on multiple representations relates to the recent emergence of technological tools—such as graphing calculators and computer software—which allow students and teachers to construct and analyze different representations efficiently (Heid et al. 1995). Recent curricular emphasis on multiple representations also relates to increasing awareness that an understanding of functions in one representation does not necessarily correspond to an understanding of them in another representation. Moreover, effective interpretation of many problem situations demands the ability to translate among varied formats (Kaput 1989; Thompson 1994). Because each representation has different limitations or strengths in different contexts, it is beneficial for students to have the choice of which representations to employ and the knowledge needed to make such choices.

As stated in Essential Understanding 5b, changing the way in which a function is represented (e.g., algebraically, with a graph, in a table, or with words) does not change the function. However, as we will discuss below, some representations of functions may be more useful than others, depending on the context in which a function is used (Essential Understanding 5c). Consider the contexts in Reflect 1.42, for example.

← ← ←

The daily operating cost for the theater, $1025 (part (*a*)), is readily available from the story, the formula, and the table (the value of *P* when *T* = 0). This precise value is more difficult to obtain from the graph because of the scale of the vertical axis. To find the number of tickets that must be sold for the theater to have a profit of $500 (part (*b*)), we are likely to choose the formula as the most efficient representation: We must solve the equation $500 = 7.5T - 1025$ for *T*. Although we can use the table and graph to get a good sense of a small range of possible values for *T*, these representations give us only partial information that we can use to answer part (*b*). The same holds for part (*c*), the "break-even point" for the theater. The constant rate of change in this function, which determines its membership in the family of linear functions, is apparent in all four of the representations: the fixed cost of tickets in the story, the slope-intercept form of the rule, the linear pattern in the graph, and the constant increases in both columns of the table. It is important for students to analyze multiple representations of the same function to develop a broad sense of the covariation between the two variables.

Essential ← Understanding 5*b*

Changing the way that a function is represented (e.g., algebraically, with a graph, in words, or with a table) does not change the function, although different representations highlight different characteristics, and some may show only part of the function.

See Reflect 1.42 on p. 80.

Essential ← Understanding 5*c*

Some representations of a function may be more useful than others, depending on the context.

Reflect 1.42

Again consider the movie theater situation presented in part (c) of Reflect 1.12. The relationship between *number of tickets sold* (*T*) and *profit* (*P*, in dollars) is represented in four different ways below.

(i) A movie theater has operating costs of $1025 per day. Tickets cost $7.50 each. The movie theater's profit each day depends on the number of tickets sold.

(ii) $P = 7.5T - 1025$

(iii)

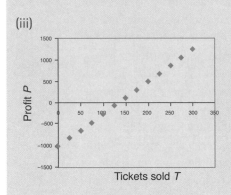

(iv)

T	P
0	– $1025
50	– $650
100	– $275
150	$100
200	$475
250	$850
300	$1225

Which of the representations above would be most helpful for determining the following information:

  a. The daily operating cost for the theater?

  b. The number of tickets that must be sold for the theater to have a profit of $500?

  c. The daily "break-even point" for the movie theater?

  d. The rate of change in the relationship?

  e. The major family of functions (e.g., linear, quadratic, exponential) to which this relationship belongs?

How does each of the pieces of information above (from (*a*) – (*e*)) appear in each of the four representations? For instance, what does the break-even point from part (c) look like on the graph? In the formula?

One way to build students' ability to recognize and connect similar patterns of change across different representations is to engage students in a "function sort" activity. As a number of authors have suggested (e.g., Cooney et al. 1996; Heid, Zbiek, and Blume 2004; Lloyd and Wilson 2002), teachers can provide students with cards depicting tables, formulas, graphs, and stories that represent members of different families of functions. As students attempt to organize the cards according to prototypical families of functions (for instance, creating one pile of cards that represents linear functions and another pile that represents quadratic functions), they must make sense of the ways that characteristic patterns of change appear in different representations. The aim of this type of activity relates closely to Essential Understanding 5b. Consider the content of the "sorting" cards shown in Reflect 1.43.

Reflect 1.43

Cooney and colleagues (1996) suggested a number of different "function sorting" tasks using a set of 28 cards, six of which are shown below. Examine the cards, and consider the following questions:

a. In what sense are cards 6, 8, and 21 alike?

b. Card 4 is to card 3 as card 21 is to what card?

3

Denise is filling a cubical container measuring one foot on each edge with water. She notices that it takes a lot more water when each dimension of the cube is increased. She wonders how much the volume of the cube increases when each dimension is increased *x* units.

4

x	-1	0	1	3	4
y	-8	-1	0	8	27

6

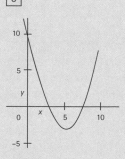

8

Fred is considering which size of pizza is a better buy. He wonders what happens to the area of the circular pizza when the diameter of the pizza is doubled.

11

Mr. Washington has noticed an increase of 3 cents per gallon in the price of regular gasoline over the past four weeks. If the current price is $1.309, he wonders what the price will be in the coming weeks if this same price increase continues each week.

21

x	-2	-1	0	1	2
y	1	0	1	4	9

Familiarity with typical characteristics of tables, graphs, and rules for prototypical function families can help students when they must solve problems that involve generating several different representations of problem situations. Reflect 1.44 presents such a problem situation.

Reflect 1.44

A gardener has 400 yards of fence to enclose a rectangular vegetable patch. Let l be the length of the vegetable patch.

  a. Write a formula for the area of the vegetable patch, A, in terms of l.

  b. Create a table of values that shows the relationship between A and l.

  c. Create a graphical representation of the relationship between A and l.

  d. Show that (80, 9600) is a point on the graph of $y = A(l)$. What meaning do these coordinates have for this problem?

  e. What are the dimensions of the vegetable patch with the greatest possible area? What point on the graph represents the maximum area?

→ **Essential Understanding 5b**

Changing the way that a function is represented (e.g., algebraically, with a graph, in words, or with a table) does not change the function, although different representations highlight different characteristics, and some may show only part of the function.

The relationship described in Reflect 1.44 can be represented by the formula $A(l) = l(200 - l)$. This formula makes sense because the area of a rectangle is a function of the length and width of the rectangle. The width of the vegetable patch is $200 - l$ because the length and width of the vegetable patch must sum to 200 yards (half of the perimeter). This formula can be used to generate a table of values and a graph to represent this situation, as shown in figure 1.40. The importance of making connections between algebraic and graphical representations of functions is Essential Understanding 5d.

Depending on the values for l chosen for the table entries, the ordered pair (80, 9600) may already appear in the table (as it does in the table in the figure). This point represents an area of 9600 square yards when the length of the vegetable patch is 80 yards. The highest point on the graph is (100, 10000). This point represents the maximum area for the vegetable patch, which occurs when the length is 100. Note that when the length is 100, the width is 100. Therefore, the largest vegetable patch results from a square design. This finding presents an interesting opportunity in the classroom to observe and discuss the connection between "squares" in geometry and "squares" in quadratics in algebra (a natural connection is that the area of an x by x square is x^2).

→ **Essential Understanding 5d**

Links between algebraic and graphical representations of functions are especially important in studying relationships and change.

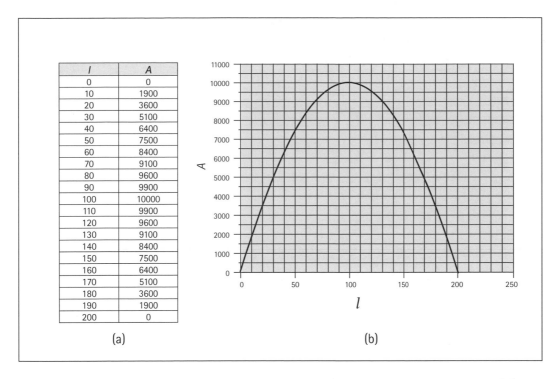

l	A
0	0
10	1900
20	3600
30	5100
40	6400
50	7500
60	8400
70	9100
80	9600
90	9900
100	10000
110	9900
120	9600
130	9100
140	8400
150	7500
160	6400
170	5100
180	3600
190	1900
200	0

(a)   (b)

Fig. 1.40. The relationship between the length and the area of the vegetable patch in (*a*) a table of values and (*b*) a graph

Connections: Looking Back and Ahead in Learning

Most of our discussion has involved the treatment of functions at the high school level. However, functions are also fundamental to mathematics in the middle grades and at the collegiate level. We address these connections in this chapter.

Functions in Middle-Grades Mathematics

Students bring a range of experiences and understandings from the middle grades to their study of functions at the high school level. Middle-grades students develop notions of variable, analyze a variety of patterns of change between variables, and represent and explore relationships by using multiple representations.

Analyzing covariation between variables

In the middle grades, students extend their elementary school experiences, now not only exploring patterns but also generalizing those patterns and developing informal notions of a *variable* as a quantity that changes. At the same time that students are making this transition, middle-grades activities should challenge them to move from the exploration of arithmetic and geometric patterns to the informal study of functions as special relationships between variables. The aim of these activities should be to introduce middle-grades students to some of the understandings related to Big Ideas 1–5.

In the middle grades, most of students' work with functions involves analyzing and representing relationships between two variables from a covariation perspective, as discussed in chapter 1. For example, relationships such as those depicted in the graphs in Reflect 2.1 can offer opportunities for students to describe how a change in one variable relates to a change in another variable (Essential Understanding 2*b*).

Essential Understanding 2*b*

A rate of change describes how one variable quantity changes with respect to another—in other words, a rate of change describes the covariation between two variables.

Reflect 2.1

Describe how the amount of water in a swimming pool (*V*, for volume) changes over time (*t*) in each case:

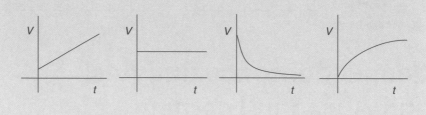

 Essential Understanding 3*a*

Members of a family of functions share the same type of rate of change. This characteristic rate of change determines the kinds of real-world phenomena that the functions in the family can model.

Reflect 2.1 asks for descriptions of changes to the *volume* of water in the pool (not the *height* of the water in the pool) over time. Students might describe the first graph as representing a scenario in which a pool is filling with water at a constant rate—as each unit of time passes, the same amount of water is added. The fourth graph also shows that the pool is filling with water; however, in this case, it is filling rapidly at first and then more slowly. The difference between these two increasing graphs allows students to recognize and articulate qualities of both *linear* and *nonlinear* relationships, thus initiating students' formal development of Essential Understanding 3*a*.

The second graph in Reflect 2.1 illustrates a *constant* function, in which the volume does not change over time; the water level in the pool remains constant. The third graph shows a decreasing relationship between *V* and *t* as water is drained from the pool, rapidly at first and then more slowly over time. By creating and examining descriptions of the graphs in this problem, middle-grades students can explore—informally and without extensive use of symbols—how and why changes occur in a particular situation.

Essential Understanding 3*b*

Linear functions are characterized by a constant rate of change. Reasoning about the similarity of "slope triangles" allows deducing that linear functions have a constant rate of change and a formula of the type f(x) = mx + b for constants m and b.

Families of functions

Although mathematics in the middle grades explores many families of functions, linear functions receive particular emphasis. Developing students' understanding of the notion that linear functions are characterized by a constant rate of change, as stated in Essential Understanding 3*b*, is a central goal of middle-grades activities. Study of linear functions builds on students' previous work with proportions. Middle-grades students are familiar with many real-world situations in which two quantities are in direct proportion, including examples such as the following:

A car is traveling at a constant speed; every 5 minutes, the car goes 3 miles.

This situation can be described by a linear function, with time t (in minutes) as input and distance d (in miles) as output. The ratio table in figure 2.1 illustrates how d increases by 3 miles as t increases by 5 minutes. The graph of this function is a line though the origin whose points (t, d) satisfy $d/t = {}^3/_5$ (or $d = {}^3/_5\,t$). The slope of this graph is ${}^3/_5$, the constant of proportionality.

Middle-grades students also examine linear functions with nonzero y-intercepts. Consider, for example, a situation in which a plain 12-inch pizza costs $6.99 and each topping costs an additional $0.80. In this situation, the price of a pizza "starts" at $6.99 and increases by $0.80 each time one topping is added. A linear function, represented in three ways (Essential Understanding 5a) as in figure 2.2, helps students to describe and understand this familiar sort of relationship that involves change between variables.

Essential Understanding 5a

Functions can be represented in various ways, including through algebraic means (e.g., equations), graphs, word descriptions, and tables.

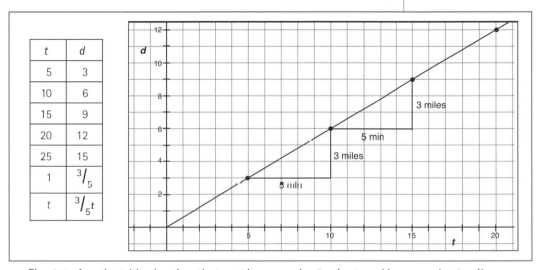

Fig. 2.1. A ratio table showing that as t increases by 5 minutes, d increases by 3 miles

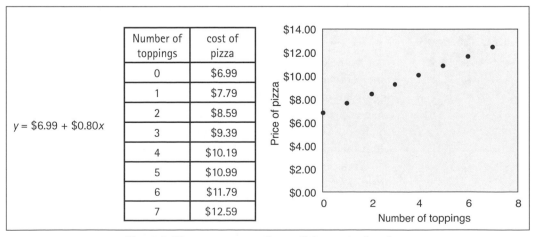

Fig. 2.2. Three representations of the cost of a pizza

Representing relationships with graphs, tables, and rules

→ Essential
Understanding 5c

*Some representations
of a function may
be more useful than
others, depending on
the context.*

→ Essential
Understanding 5b

*Changing the way
that a function is
represented (e.g.,
algebraically, with
a graph, in words, or
with a table) does not
change the function,
although different
representations
highlight different
characteristics, and
some may show only
part of the function.*

See Reflect 2.2
on p. 89.

In the middle grades, students begin to recognize the usefulness of different representations—particularly graphs, tables, and algebraic rules (Essential Understanding 5c). For example, in the pizza situation, the table allows students to arrive at answers quickly to such questions as, "How many toppings are on a pizza that costs $9.39?" However, the algebraic rule provides the most efficient tool for generating particular input-output pairs (e.g., the cost of a pizza with 4 toppings). The graph offers a clear picture of the linear nature of the relationship between number of toppings and cost. Although the points on the graph in figure 2.2 are not connected, they do lie on a line. Middle-grades students should discuss why the points on such a graph are not connected—it makes sense to talk only about whole numbers of pizza toppings. Students may question the relevance of using large numbers of toppings or raise the possibility of half toppings (that is, toppings that cover only half of the pizza), and doing so reflects a legitimate effort to constrain or extend the domain of this function.

Middle-grades activities also help students to observe how the same characteristics of a particular function can be determined through analysis of different representations (Essential Understanding 5b). In the pizza situation, the y-intercept of the graph corresponds to the first entry of the table, when no toppings are added to the pizza. Middle-grades students would also consider how the rate of change is evident in the table, graph, and algebraic formula. These experiences can help students to understand the slope-intercept form of a line, which can sometimes lack meaning for students.

Consider Reflect 2.2, which presents a growing pattern of squares. An important goal in the middle grades is to revisit and generalize patterns explored in the elementary grades, such as the geometric pattern shown.

→   →   →

In the elementary grades, students typically describe this pattern with words and numbers and continue the pattern by drawing or building with colored tiles. In the middle grades, students are equipped to describe changes to the perimeter and area of the squares in the pattern. Their representations of these relationships often include a table, graph, and formulas, as shown in figure 2.3.

As students create these representations, important questions arise: Does it make sense to connect the points on the graph? What is the meaning of the numbers on the y-axis when area and perimeter are graphed together (since area and perimeter are measured with different units)? These different representations allow students to

Reflect 2.2

The geometric pattern below contains several different numeric sequences. Each large square is comprised of unit squares.

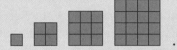

Consider the pattern in the *perimeters* of the large squares in the sequence. To do so, create a table, graph, and equation that represent the relationship between perimeter and position in the sequence (which is the same as the side length of the square). Use these representations together to describe changes in a square's perimeter relative to its side length.

Create representations of the *area* relationship in the sequence. How does the area of a square relate to its side length? Use multiple representations to explore this question.

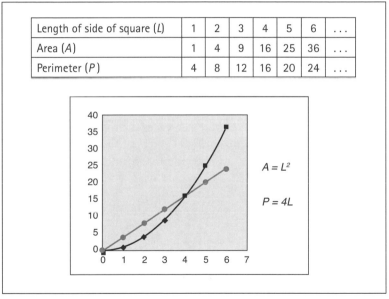

Length of side of square (L)	1	2	3	4	5	6	. . .
Area (A)	1	4	9	16	25	36	. . .
Perimeter (P)	4	8	12	16	20	24	. . .

$A = L^2$

$P = 4L$

Fig. 2.3. A table, graph, and rules to show the relationship between the side length of a square and its perimeter and area

identify specific information about the two relationships—namely, the perimeter and area of a square with a given side length. Students also learn to describe the covariation between side length and perimeter and between side length and area in terms of the different rates of change in the two relationships. Whereas the perimeter function exhibits a constant rate of change, the rate of change in the area function *changes* as the sequence progresses. In addition, students' ability to use the graph and table to identify the points at which perimeter and area have the same numerical value lays conceptual groundwork for solving algebraic equations.

Much of what students learn about functions in grades 9–12 draws on the ideas and understandings that emerge from problems of the sort discussed in this section. For example, experiences in the middle grades with linear and nonlinear functions in different representations lead to the analysis and classification of many function families in high school. Ultimately, middle-grades experiences should prepare students to use functions as tools to understand and describe change in diverse real-world and mathematical situations.

Connections to Collegiate Studies

One theme that we have examined is that the members of a family of functions share not only the same type of formula, but they also share a characteristic pattern of change. At the college level, the study of "the way functions change" takes place in differential calculus, integral calculus, and differential equations.

Differential equations

A differential equation is an equation that relates a function with some of its derivatives (such as the first or second derivative). For example, Newton's law of cooling states that if $T(t)$ is the temperature of a hot liquid t seconds after it is poured into a container, then the rate at which the temperature decreases is proportional to the difference between the temperature of the liquid and the ambient room temperature. Reflect 2.3 asks you to consider this proportional relationship.

Reflect 2.3

Try to formulate Newton's law of cooling with an equation that involves $T(t)$, its derivative $T'(t)$, the ambient room temperature A, and a constant of proportionality k.

The difference between the temperature of the liquid and the ambient room temperature is $T(t) - A$. A quantity that is proportional to this difference is of the form $k \cdot (T(t) - A)$ for some constant k (which depends on how well or poorly the container insulates the liquid). Because the rate at which the temperature changes is the derivative of the temperature function, the temperature function must satisfy the differential equation $T'(t) = -k \cdot (T(t) - A)$. Why is there a negative sign (assuming k is positive)? The temperature is decreasing, so the rate of change of the temperature function is negative. It turns out that the temperature functions that solve this differential equation are of the form $T(t) = A + Be^{-kt}$, where B is any positive constant.

Extending domains of functions to the complex numbers

In high school, students learn that complex numbers are the numbers that can be written in the form $a + ib$, where a and b are real numbers and i denotes a square root of –1. Students also learn to write complex numbers in "polar form" as $r(\cos(\theta) + i\sin(\theta))$, where r is a nonnegative real number and θ is a real number. The classical functions—such as polynomials, rational functions, exponential functions, logarithmic functions, and trigonometric functions—can all be extended so that their domains are (or lie within) the complex numbers instead of just the real numbers. The most interesting case is probably the way in which we extend the exponential function e^x. Because we still want the usual rules of exponents to work, we want it to be the case that $e^{x+iy} = e^x \cdot e^{iy}$. Therefore, to extend the exponential function to the complex numbers, we really need only to say how $e^{i\theta}$ is defined, where θ is a real number. According to an amazing theorem called *Euler's formula*, $e^{i\theta} = \cos(\theta) + i\sin(\theta)$. So, for example, $e^{i\pi} = -1$ because $\cos(\pi) = -1$ and $\sin(\pi) = 0$. In light of the fact that $e = 2.718...$, $\pi = 3.141...$, and i is a square root of –1, it is quite astounding that these numbers are connected in this way!

For the rules of exponents to work, we should expect that $e^{i(A+B)} = e^{iA} \cdot e^{iB}$. Reflect 2.4 suggests a way to investigate this situation.

Reflect 2.4

Reformulate the equation $e^{i(A+B)} = e^{iA} \cdot e^{iB}$ in terms of cosine and sine, and explain why the equation must be true.

We can reformulate the equation as

$$\cos(A + B) + i\sin(A + B) = (\cos(A) + i\sin(A)) \cdot (\cos(B) + i\sin(B)).$$

If we multiply the right side and collect the real part and the imaginary part, keeping in mind that $i^2 = -1$, we find that the equation must be true because of the formulas for the cosine and sine of a sum of angles. In fact, the equation $e^{i(A+B)} = e^{iA} \cdot e^{iB}$ provides a convenient way to recover the formulas for the cosine and sine of a sum of angles, should you happen to forget them.

But why would anyone think of relating $e^{i\theta}$ to cosine and sine? We can see the connection among these functions by considering the Taylor expansions of e^x, $\cos(x)$, and $\sin(x)$. It turns out that

$$e^x = 1 + \frac{x}{1!} + \frac{x^2}{2!} + \frac{x^3}{3!} + \frac{x^4}{4!} + \frac{x^5}{5!} \cdots$$

$$\cos(x) = 1 - \frac{x^2}{2!} + \frac{x^4}{4!} - \frac{x^6}{6!} + \cdots$$

$$\sin(x) = \frac{x}{1!} - \frac{x^3}{3!} + \frac{x^5}{5!} - \frac{x^7}{7!} + \cdots$$

If we formally substitute ix for x in the Taylor expansion for e^x and collect the real and imaginary parts, we can see why e^{ix} should be related to cosine and sine.

The examples here provide just a very small taste of some ways in which the study of functions continues in college mathematics courses and beyond. Indeed, the study of functions pervades all of modern mathematics.

Chapter 3

Challenges: Learning, Teaching, and Assessing

What have we learned about the difficulties that students encounter in learning about functions? What implications do these learning difficulties have for teaching? In this section, we consider some difficulties that students face when learning about the function concept, the role of functions in understanding real-world phenomena, and the interplay between functions and their graphical representations.

The Concept of Function

Big Idea 1 (the function concept) points to the importance of students' appreciating the wide range of situations modeled by functions and being able to distinguish functions from nonfunctions. Leinhardt, Zaslavsky, and Stein (1990), in their review of students' understanding of functions, pointed out that students' early experiences with functions are often limited to easily recognizable patterns that involve linearity or symmetry and working with the single-valued criterion for functions. Students seldom have difficulty sorting out functions from nonfunctions, given sets of ordered pairs. Typically, middle school students can successfully answer questions such as the following:

> Choose a value for *a* so that the following relation is *not* a function: {(1, 2), (2, 4), (3, 6), (*a*, 8)}. Explain why it is not a function.

Yet, as noted by Leinhardt and colleagues, many students have difficulty recognizing that many-to-one correspondences, including constant functions, also constitute functions. Although students appreciate the single-valued criterion for functions, they often interpret it as synonymous with a one-to-one criterion. It is also the

Big Idea 1

The function concept

The concept of function is intentionally broad and flexible, allowing it to apply to a wide range of situations. The notion of function encompasses many types of mathematical entities in addition to "classical" functions that describe quantities that vary continuously. For example, matrices and arithmetic and geometric sequences can be viewed as functions.

case that students may not recognize that relationships that do not follow "neat" rules or that involve nonnumerical relationships can also be functions (Even 1990).

Thompson (1994) noted that students have a predominant image of functions as "two written expressions separated by an equal sign" (p. 24). Similarly, Breidenbach and colleagues (1992) found that when students were asked to give examples of functions, nearly two-thirds of them equated "$f(x)$" or "y" with some algebraic or trigonometric expression, suggesting to the researchers that students tend to view functions as equations. Furthermore, the majority of students thought of a function as a mathematical entity that calls for substituting numbers for variables and calculating the result. Such limited orientations preclude an appreciation of different algebraic representations (e.g.,

$$\sum_{n=1}^{N} (2n - 1),$$

as opposed to the more familiar $f(x) = x^2$). They also ignore functional representations that include tables, graphs, and word descriptions. As noted by Breidenbach and colleagues, a conception of function as an equation can lead to an emphasis on functions as calculations. Such a perspective is not broad enough or sufficiently flexible to allow for thinking of functions as vehicles for representing real-world phenomena or for understanding the transformations of functions.

Related to an understanding of the concept of function is the propensity of students to "see" relationships in linear terms, whether or not the situation calls for a linear relationship. Heid, Zbiek, and Blume (2004) described a classroom discussion of a situation involving exponential growth (population growth) in which students were given the populations at the ends of weeks 1 and 3 and asked to estimate the population at the end of week 2. The teacher found that some students estimated the week 2 population by identifying the value that was halfway between the values for weeks 1 and 3— a method that would have worked for a linear situation. A similar example was reported by Leinhardt and colleagues (1990), who found that when students were given two points on a graph and asked to draw the graph of a function containing the two points, they generally drew a straight line containing the two points and failed to consider the possibility that other functions might also contain the two given points. A lack of appreciation for the behavior of nonlinear functions can lead to misconceptions, especially when estimating or interpolating on the basis of given data. Reflect 3.1 emphasizes such a misconception.

Reflect 3.1

Jackie has been offered a job at a local company. She has been told that beginning employees start at an annual salary of $50,000, that their salary increases 4% per year, and that after 10 years their salary is $74,012. Jackie predicts that if she takes the job, her salary after 5 years will be $62,006.

How do you think Jackie arrived at her prediction of $62,006?

On the basis of the information that Jackie was given, do you think that she has correctly predicted her salary after 5 years?

Functions as Models for Real-World Phenomena

Big Idea 3
Families of functions

Functions can be classified into different families of functions, each with its own unique characteristics. Different families can be used to model different real-world phenomena.

Big Idea 3 (families of functions) emphasizes the unique characteristics of different families of functions and the role that those characteristics play in modeling real-world phenomena. However, several challenges are associated with students acquiring the essential understandings associated with this big idea. Generally speaking, there is a disconnect between students' mathematical experiences and their real-world experiences. Because students see these two domains of experience as separate from one another, it is difficult for them to appreciate the role that functions can play in modeling real-world phenomena.

A study by Janvier (1978) highlights the kinds of difficulties that students have. Janvier noted students' confusion between the slope and the height of graphs that represent real-world phenomena. For example, students were given graph A shown in figure 3.1 and told that it represented a wide jar being filled with water. They were then asked what the graph might look like if a narrower jar were filled with water poured at the same rate. Instead of drawing a graph like C, the correct graph, most students drew a graph like B. They recognized that the height should be higher but failed to realize the necessity of having a graph with an increased slope.

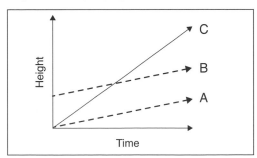

Fig. 3.1. Graph A shows the height of water filling a wide jar; students typically drew a graph like B instead of one like C to show a narrower jar filling at the same rate.

Students often have difficulty with the idea that a change in one condition can affect graphs in multiple ways—in this case, affecting both the height and the slope of the graph. Reflect 3.2 asks you to consider approaches that might clarify students' ideas.

> **Reflect 3.2**
>
> What question(s) would you pose to help students understand that a graph like C is the correct graph?

Boaler (1999) focused on the considerable difficulties that students have in connecting mathematics and real-world phenomena because of their lack of experience in making those connections. Perhaps the problem is compounded by the fact that students often see mathematics as an abstract subject that seldom intersects with their lives apart from academic ventures. Whatever the reasons, it seems clear that classroom activities and discussions need to place a greater emphasis on connecting functions to real-world phenomena, either through problems to be solved or through more explicit references to how functions can facilitate quantitative thinking.

 Big Idea 5
Multiple represent-ations of functions

Functions can be represented in multiple ways, including algebraic (symbolic), graphical, verbal, and tabular representations. Links among these different representa-tions are important to studying relation-ships and change.

Graphical and Algebraic Representations of Functions

Big Idea 5 (multiple representations of functions) emphasizes the various ways in which functions can be represented. It is important that students develop flexibility in shifting between algebraic representations and other types of representations. Although students are often adept at graphing functions, especially when using appropriate technologies, they are less adept at identifying a reasonable algebraic representation when given a graphical representation. To highlight this difficulty, consider the problem (Cooney et al. 2002) in Reflect 3.3.

See Reflect 3.3 on p. 97.

Three students who were given the problem provided the answers shown in figure 3.2. It appears that the students had difficulty in dealing with the full complexity of the problem; rather, they each focused on a limited aspect of it. For example, the first student understood that the expected graph is (most likely) a parabola but failed to take into consideration the y-intercept. By contrast, the second student focused on the y-intercept to the exclusion of the information about x-intercepts. The third student understood the y-intercept and the fact that the graph should probably be a parabola but apparently assumed that $f(x) = x^2 + 3$ meets the criterion of intersecting the x-axis twice.

Reflect 3.3

Suppose that you gave your students the following problem:

> If you were to zoom out on the graph below, you would see that it has exactly two x-intercepts. Write an equation of a function that would fit the criterion. Explain why your equation fits the criterion.

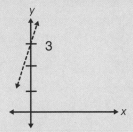

What various responses might you expect from your students?

Student 1

$y = (x + 4)(x + 9)$

the graph is a parabola with x-int
x = -4 and -9.

Student 2

$y = 3$

The line passes through point 3 on the y axis

Student 3

$x^2 + 3$

3 would be the y-intercept
x^2 means it crosses the x-axis twice.

Fig. 3.2. Three students' responses to the problem in Reflect 3.3

Had the students been asked to graph $y = x^2 + 4x + 3$ (which would satisfy the criterion), it is likely they would have encountered little difficulty. But when the problem became more complex by showing only part of the graph with an associated criterion, they experienced considerable difficulty. Students' experiences with graphs typically begin with a symbolic representation and move to the graphical, instead of proceeding the other way around, as in the preceding problem.

Even (1990) identified several difficulties that prospective secondary mathematics teachers had in understanding functions.

They understood, for example, that if a parabola represented by $f(x) = ax^2 + bx + c$ opens down, then it must have a negative a-value. Yet, they were unable to provide a meaningful explanation of why this must be the case. Informally, we can argue that since the x^2 term grows faster than either the x or the constant term, then the x^2 term "wins out," and consequently the graph either becomes "more negative" or "more positive," depending on the value of a. If your students made this informal argument, would you find it sufficient? Reflect 3.4 probes your thinking.

Reflect 3.4

How formal an explanation would you want your students to provide in response to the question about why a parabola opens up or down, depending on the coefficient of the x^2 term?

Another difficulty that students have in dealing with graphical representations is their lack of attention to the domain and range of a function. For example, students seldom distinguish the graphical representations of a function of the form $f(x) = ax + b$ when, in one case, the domain and range are the set of real numbers and, in another case, the domain and range are the set of integers or natural numbers. Recall the pizza problem posed in chapter 2 about a 12-inch pizza costing $6.99, with each additional topping costing $0.80 (see page 87). How would students draw this graph, and what would they consider a reasonable domain to be? We pointed out earlier that the domain is likely to be whole numbers (probably ranging from 1 to 10), or possibly "halves" to reflect "half toppings," but clearly not the set of real numbers. Although it may not be a serious problem if students draw a continuous line that represents the pizza topping-cost relationship, they should nevertheless be aware that, with respect to the domain, only certain numbers make sense when they are interpreting the graph.

Assessing Big Ideas and Essential Understandings

Much has been written over the past several decades about assessing students' understanding of mathematics. We will not review those discussions, but we would like to make several points about assessing students' understanding of functions. First, it is important to keep in mind that assessment is about obtaining information about students' thinking and trying to discern the extent to which they understand functions. Second, it is important to realize that any attempt to assess such understanding necessarily entails taking a sample of that understanding. A physician, when conducting a medical examination, takes a sample of blood—not all the patient's blood—for analysis. Similarly, our questions, whether they are true-false, multiple-choice, open-ended, or essay, provide a basis for obtaining a sample of what the student knows and understands. Consequently, it is important that our sample provide the kind of information that we value in deciding what students understand about functions.

We have focused on five big ideas and associated essential understandings that embody what we expect students to understand. Specifically, we want students to understand (1) what distinguishes functions from other mathematical entities, (2) how rates of change characterize various kinds of functions, (3) how functions can be classified into families with shared characteristics that are useful in modeling real-world phenomena, (4) how functions can be combined or transformed to create new functions, and (5) how functions can be represented in a variety of ways in which relationships and change can be examined. In this section, we offer tools for constructing assessment items that help to assess students' understanding of these big ideas.

Students are often asked questions such as the following, which provide a basis for gathering information about their understanding of linear and quadratic functions but may fail to address the big ideas and essential understandings previously discussed:

Write an equation of a line that contains the points (0, 3) and (2, 7).

For the quadratic function $y = 3(x - 1)^2 + 5$, find the vertex of the graph and state whether the graph opens up or down.

Although it is important for students to be able to complete tasks such as these successfully, it is critical that they develop an ability to move fluidly among the five big ideas so that they can go beyond these more routine tasks. Students need to develop the ability to move easily among the many interpretations of functions, their characteristics, and the way in which they can be used to represent real-world phenomena. To assess these kinds of outcomes, it is imperative that questions be posed that allow students to demonstrate that fluency. We offer two means by which such questions can be generated, as well as suggestions for assessing students' responses that focus on various aspects of functions.

Extending problems

One of the techniques that teachers can use to gather information about students' understanding is to pose questions that extend given problems and require students to think beyond them. For example, consider the problem posed in Reflect 2.2, which called for developing an expression that connected the sequence $x = 1, 2, 3, 4, \ldots$ and the perimeter and the area of the given figures. These expressions were $P = 4x$ and $A = x^2$. The following question, although perhaps nonsensical from a real-world perspective, can nonetheless lead to some interesting investigations involving relationships:

> For what value of x would the perimeter and the area have the same numerical value?

Now, let's extend the problem and consider the same relationships for 1×2 rectangles, as shown in figure 3.3. Reflect 3.5 explores the relationship between x and the perimeter and area of the various configurations.

$x = 1$ $x = 2$ $x = 3$ $x = 4$

Fig. 3.3. A sequence of shapes composed of 1 × 2 rectangles

Reflect 3.5

Construct a table, graph, and equation that express the relationship between x and the perimeters of the figures.

Construct a table, graph, and equation that express the relationship between x and the areas of the figures.

Is there a value for x for which the perimeter and the area have the same numerical value?

How did the relationships change? Suppose that the rectangles had measures 1×3, not 1×2. How would these relationships then change? Is it always the case that whatever the size of the rectangle, there will be some x-value for which the perimeter and the area will have the same numerical value? Examination of these questions provides a context for considering not only relationships between perimeter and area but also how those relationships might change when different-sized rectangles are considered.

A related question is whether the relationships would change if the figures in Reflect 2.2 had been 2×2 or 3×3 and not unit squares. Would the relationships expressed in the equation remain the same? Would the x-value that yielded the same numerical values for the perimeter and area change if the squares had been assigned some dimension other than unit squares? These extensions can provide an opportunity for students to demonstrate their ability to interpret and reinterpret their understanding of area and perimeter as functions in increasingly complicated situations. Consider, for example, what the relationships might be if the rectangles were l by w rather than specific measures.

Another extension involves the often-encountered "biggest box" problem, a version of which is stated in figure 3.4. We leave it to the reader to verify that the volume of the box can be expressed by the equation $V = x(20 - 2x)^2$ and that the largest volume of the box is $592\,^{16}/_{27}$ square centimeters when $x = 3^1/_3$ centimeters. The graph of the relationship is shown in figure 3.5.

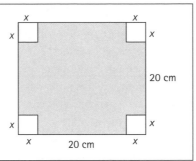

Suppose squares of dimension x by x are cut from each corner of the 20-by-20 square and the subsequent shape is folded to make a (topless) box. What value of x would yield the greatest volume, and what would that volume be?

Fig. 3.4. The "biggest box" problem

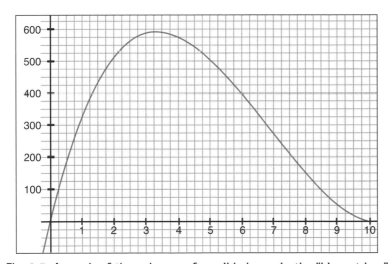

Fig. 3.5. A graph of the volumes of possible boxes in the "biggest box" problem

In this version of the biggest box problem, the surface area of the topless box is 20×20 reduced by $4x^2$. Now, suppose that the $4x^2$ could be redistributed to increase the sides of the box (for example, imagine that the box were made out of metal that could be melted and reformed). In this case, the area of each side of the topless box would increase by an amount equal to x^2. In short, the box would then have the same surface area (400 sq. cm) as the original sheet. In light of this extension, consider the questions in Reflect 3.6.

Reflect 3.6

Construct an equation, table, and graph that express the relationship between *x* and the volume of the topless box, assuming that its surface area remains constant (400 sq. cm).

What value of *x* yields the topless box with the largest volume? Is it the same *x*-value that yielded the biggest box in the original problem?

Reversing problems

Another way to create problems to assess students' understanding is to "reverse" a problem. For example, instead of asking students to graph an equation, you can ask them to write an equation that corresponds to a given graph. Alternatively, instead of asking students to solve an equation, you can ask them to write an equation that would have the given roots. Typically, students are asked to graph equations such as $y = x^2$, $y = x^2 - 3$, and $y = (x + 3)^2$ to develop an understanding of how different parameters affect graphs. The problem posed in Reflect 3.7 represents the reverse of graphing particular equations.

This problem offers students an opportunity to demonstrate their ability to move back and forth between graphical and algebraic representations of functions. In particular, students might move among various transformations—some scalar, some translations—of graphs of functions. As a result, the problem provides a vehicle for assessing students' understanding of at least some aspects of Big Ideas 4 and 5.

An example of a "reversed" problem can be generated from a fact that we previously established: Every arithmetic sequence can be viewed as a linear function (whose domain is the positive integers). Reflect 3.8 shows such a "reversed" problem, which cuts across several essential understandings.

See Reflect 3.7
on p. 103.

Big Idea 4
Combining and trans-forming functions

Functions can be combined by adding, subtracting, multiplying, dividing, and composing them. Functions sometimes have inverses. Functions can often be analyzed by viewing them as made from other functions.

Reflect 3.8

Is it possible to create a linear function that is not an arithmetic sequence when its domain is restricted to the positive integers? If yes, create such a linear function. If no, explain why it is not possible.

Problems of the sort suggested in this section can challenge students to demonstrate the extent to which they can move between one kind of understanding and another. Such fluency is indispensable for students to develop an understanding of the big ideas and associated essential understandings emphasized in this book.

Reflect 3.7

Consider the following graph of $y = f(x)$.

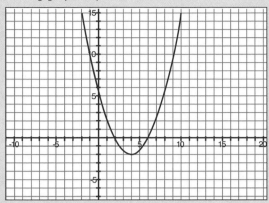

Select among the following six equations and label the four graphs below. Justify your selection for each graph.

$$y = f(x + 3) \qquad y = f(x) + 3 \qquad y = 3f(x)$$
$$y = f(x) - 3 \qquad y = f(x - 3) \qquad y = f(3x)$$

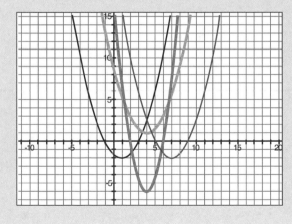

Big Idea 5
Multiple representations of functions

Functions can be represented in multiple ways, including algebraic (symbolic), graphical, verbal, and tabular representations. Links among these different representations are important to studying relationships and change.

Assessing Outcomes

Unless a question is of the yes-no or true-false type, there is always room for interpretation of students' responses to it. We will not address the construction of rubrics and their applications here, but we do want to emphasize the importance of attending to and assessing a range of students' understanding in other than dichotomous (all right vs. all wrong) terms. Common sense suggests that students' responses to a non-dichotomous question will fall into the following general categories: virtually nothing is correct, some but not many things are correct, most but not all things are correct (including explanations), the explanations are clear and correct. In light of these common-sense notions, we offer the following four-point rubric (see Cooney et al. [2002]):

  0: Response indicates no appropriate mathematical reasoning.

  1: Response indicates some mathematical reasoning but fails to address the item's main mathematical ideas.

  2: Response indicates substantial and appropriate mathematical reasoning but is lacking in some minor way(s).

  3: Response is correct, and the underlying reasoning process is appropriate and clearly communicated.

Consider the actual student responses shown in figure 3.6 to the following problem on function composition (see Cooney et al. [2002]):

Identify 2 distinct functions f and g such that $f(g(x)) = g(f(x))$. Explain why your functions satisfy the condition.

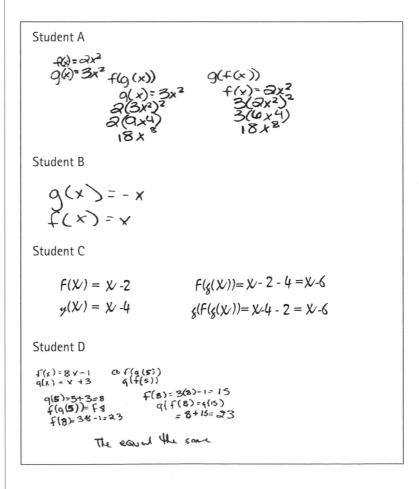

Fig. 3.6. Students' work in identifying two functions f and g such that
$f(g(x)) = g(f(x))$

What aspects of the problem do these four students seem to understand or not understand? Student A has some idea about function composition but fails to compose the functions correctly. Student B provides functions that satisfy the condition but offers no explanation. Student C demonstrates some understanding of function composition but is confused between $f(x)$ and $g(x)$. Student D seems to think that function composition is a matter of generating a number, a common misunderstanding that we pointed out earlier in students' conceptions of function. How would you evaluate these responses according to our suggested 4-point rubric? This is the question that Reflect 3.9 investigates.

Reflect 3.9

Using the 0-1-2-3 rubric presented in this section, what score would you assign to each of the students' responses in figure 3.6? Explain why you assigned the scores that you did.

Which big idea(s) do you think the problem best assesses? What follow-up questions might you ask students to gain a better understanding of their thinking?

Now go back and reconsider the student responses that figure 3.2 shows to the problem in Reflect 3.3. In light of these responses from students, consider the questions posed in Reflect 3.10.

Reflect 3.10

Using the 0-1-2-3 rubric presented in this section, what score would you assign to each of the students' responses in figure 3.2 to the problem presented in Reflect 3.3? Explain why you assigned the scores that you did.

Which big idea(s) do you think that the problem best assesses? What follow-up questions might you ask students to access their thinking?

In this section, we have discussed numerous ways of assessing students' understandings of functions. Some of the Reflect questions presented in earlier sections of the book also offer sample tasks that you might use or adapt to assess your students' knowledge about the big ideas and associated essential understandings explored in this book. We note that many effective assessment tasks will address more than one big idea, as do many of the Reflect questions posed throughout this book.

Assessing students' understanding of big ideas about functions involves at least two components. First, students must be offered opportunities for demonstrating that understanding. In the absence of questions that demand such understanding, one never knows the extent to which they do or do not possess essential understandings about functions. Second, it is imperative that students be provided feedback on the level of their understanding. One means of doing this is to show students examples of level 3 responses so that they can develop an appreciation for what it means to provide a complete and accurate explanation. Students need visions of what is possible so that they can take responsibility for deepening their own understanding of functions.

References

Boaler, Jo. "Participation, Knowledge, and Beliefs: A Community Perspective on Mathematical Learning." *Educational Studies in Mathematics* 40 (December 1999): 259–81.

Breidenbach, Daniel, Ed Dubinsky, Julie Hawks, and Devilyna Nichols. "Development of the Process Conception of Function." *Educational Studies in Mathematics* 23 (June 1992): 247–85.

Carlson, Marilyn, and Michael Oehrtman. "Key Aspects of Knowing and Learning the Concept of Function." *MAA Online*, March 15, 2005, http://www.maa.org/t_and_l/sampler/rs_9.html.

Confrey, Jere, and Erick Smith. "Exponential Functions, Rate of Change, and the Multiplicative Unit." *Educational Studies in Mathematics* 26 (March 1994): 135–64.

———. "Splitting, Covariation, and Their Role in the Development of Exponential Functions." *Journal for Research in Mathematics Education* 26 (January 1995): 66–86.

Cooney, Thomas, Stephen I. Brown, John A. Dossey, Georg Schrage, and Erich Ch. Wittmann. *Mathematics, Pedagogy, and Secondary Teacher Education.* Portsmouth, N.H.: Heinemann, 1996.

Cooney, Thomas, Wendy B. Sanchez, Keith Leatham, and Denise S. Mewborn. *Open-Ended Assessment in Math: A Searchable Collection of 450+ Questions.* Portsmouth, N.H.: Heinemann, 2002. www.heinemann.com/math.

Edwards, C. Henry, and David E. Penney. *Calculus: Early Transcendentals, Matrix Version.* 6th ed. Upper Saddle River, N.J.: Prentice Hall, 2002.

Even, Ruhama. "Subject Matter Knowledge for Teaching and the Case of Functions." *Educational Studies in Mathematics* 21 (December 1990): 521–44.

Fernandez, Eileen. "Understanding Functions without Using the Vertical Line Test." *Mathematics Teacher* 99 (September 2005): 96–100.

Freudenthal, Hans. *Didactical Phenomenology of Mathematical Structures.* Dordrecht, The Netherlands: D. Reidel, 1983.

Heid, M. Kathleen, Jonathan Choate, Charleen Sheets, and Rose Mary Zbiek. *Algebra in a Technological World.* Reston, Va.: National Council of Teachers of Mathematics, 1995.

Heid, M. Kathleen, Rose Mary Zbiek, and Glendon W. Blume. "Mathematical Foundations for a Functions-Based Approach to Algebra." In *Perspectives on Teaching Mathematics*, 2004 Yearbook of the National Council of Teachers of Mathematics (NCTM), edited by Rheta N. Rubenstein, pp. 42–55. Reston, Va.: NCTM, 2004.

Hill, Richard. "What (Future) High School Math Teachers Need to
      Know about Trigonometry." http://www.math.msu.edu/~hill
      /TeachersTrig.pdf.

Holliday, Berchie, Gilbert J. Cuevas, Beatrice Moore-Harris, John A.
      Carter, Daniel Marks, Ruth M. Casey, Roger Day, and Linda M.
      Hayek. *Algebra 1*. New York: Glencoe/McGraw Hill, 2005.

Hughes-Hallet, Deborah, Andrew M. Gleason, and Daniel E. Flath.
      Calculus. Hoboken, N.J.: John Wiley and Sons, 1994.

Interactive Mathematics Program. *The World of Functions*. Teacher's
      Guide, Year 4. Emeryville, Calif.: Key Curriculum Press, 2000.

Janvier, Claude. "The Interpretation of Complex Cartesian Graphs
      Representing Situations—Studies and Teaching Experiences."
      Ph.D. diss., University of Nottingham, 1978.

Kaput, James J. "Linking Representations in the Symbol System
      of Algebra." In *Research Issues in the Learning and Teaching
      of Algebra,* edited by Sigrid Wagner and Carolyn Kieran, pp.
      167–94, vol. 4, Research Agenda for Mathematics Education.
      Reston, Va.: National Council of Teachers of Mathematics, 1989.

Klein, Felix. *Elementary Mathematics from an Advanced Standpoint*.
      New York: Dover, 1945.

Leinhardt, Gaea, Orit Zaslavsky, and Mary Kay Stein. "Functions,
      Graphs, and Graphing: Tasks, Learning, and Teaching." *Review
      of Educational Research* 60 (Spring 1990): 1–64.

Lloyd, Gwendolyn M., and Melvin (Skip) Wilson. "Using a Card Sort
      to Determine One's Understanding of Function." In *Lessons
      Learned from Research*, edited by Judith Sowder and Bonnie
      Schappelle, pp. 209–12. Reston, Va.: National Council of Teach-
      ers of Mathematics, 2002.

National Council of Teachers of Mathematics (NCTM). *Curriculum
      and Evaluation Standards for School Mathematics*. Reston, Va.:
      NCTM, 1989.

———. *Principles and Standards for School Mathematics*. Reston,
      Va.: NCTM, 2000.

———. *Curriculum Focal Points for Prekindergarten through Grade 8
      Mathematics: A Quest for Coherence*. Reston, Va.: NCTM, 2006.

———. *Focus in High School Mathematics: Reasoning and Sense
      Making*. Reston, Va.: NCTM, 2009.

Saxon, John H. *Advanced Mathematics: An Incremental Approach*.
      2nd ed. Norman, Okla.: Saxon, 2003.

Silverman, Joseph A. *A Friendly Introduction to Number Theory*.
      Upper Saddle River, N.J.: Prentice Hall, 1997.

Smith, Erick. "Stasis and Change: Integrating Patterns, Functions,
      and Algebra throughout the K–12 Curriculum." In *A Research
      Companion to "Principles and Standards for School Mathemat-
      ics,"* edited by Jeremy Kilpatrick, W. Gary Martin, and Deborah

Schifter, pp. 136–50. Reston, Va.: National Council of Teachers of Mathematics, 2003.

Thompson, Patrick W. "Students, Functions, and the Undergraduate Curriculum." In *Research in Collegiate Mathematics Education*, edited by Ed Dubinsky, Alan H. Schoenfeld, and Jim Kaput, pp. 21-44, vol. 4, CBMS Issues in Mathematics Education. Providence, R.I.: American Mathematical Society, 1994.

Usiskin, Zalman, Anthony L. Peressini, Elena Marchisotto, and Dick Stanley. *Mathematics for High School Teachers: An Advanced Perspective.* Upper Saddle River, N.J.: Pearson Education, 2003.

Titles in the Essential Understanding Series

The Essential Understanding Series gives teachers the deep understanding that they need to teach challenging topics in mathematics. Students encounter such topics across the pre-K–grade 12 curriculum, and teachers who understand the related big ideas can give maximum support as students develop their own understanding and make vital connections.

Visit www.nctm.org/catalog for details and ordering information.